**BIENNALE
ARCHITETTURA
2021**

How will we live together?

D1620710

**PARTICIPATING COUNTRIES
AND COLLATERAL EVENTS**

Contents

BIENNALE
ARCHITETTURA
2021
PARTICIPATING COUNTRIES
AND COLLATERAL EVENTS

**PARTICIPATING
COUNTRIES**

6   Albania

8   Argentina

10   Republic of Armenia

12   Australia

14   Austria

16   Republic of Azerbaijan

18   Kingdom of Bahrain

20   Belgium

22   Brazil

24   Canada

26   Chile

28   People's Republic of China

30   Croatia

32   Republic of Cyprus

34   Denmark

36   Dominican Republic

38   Egypt

40   Estonia

42   Finland

44   France

46   Germany

48   Great Britain

50   Greece

52   Grenada

54   Hungary

56   Iraq

58   Ireland

60   Israel

62   Italy

68   Japan

70   Republic of Korea

72   Republic of Kosovo

74   Kuwait

76   Latvia

78   Lebanon

80   Lithuania

82   Grand Duchy of Luxembourg

84   Republic of
North Macedonia

86   Mexico

88   Montenegro

90   The Netherlands

92   Nordic Countries
Norway-Sweden-Finland

94 Pakistan

96 Peru

98 Philippines

100 Poland

102 Portugal

104 Romania

106 Russia

108 Republic of San Marino

110 Saudi Arabia

112 Serbia

114 Singapore

116 Republic of Slovenia

118 Spain

120 Switzerland

122 Thailand

124 Turkey

126 United Arab Emirates

128 United States of America

130 Uruguay

132 Republic of Uzbekistan

134 Padiglione Venezia

SPECIAL PROJECT PAVILION OF APPLIED ARTS

140 Three British Mosques

COLLATERAL EVENTS

146 Air/Aria/Aire_Catalonia in Venice

148 'Charlotte Perriand and I'. Converging designs by Frank Gehry and Charlotte Perriand

150 Connectivities: Living beyond the boundaries – Macao and the Greater Bay Area

152 Hakka Earthen Houses on variation-Co-operative Living, Art and Migration Architecture in China

154 Lianghekou

156 Mutualities

158 Not Vital. SCARCH

160 Primitive Migration from/to Taiwan

162 Redistribution: Land, People & Environment

164 Revive the Spirit of Mosul

166 *Salon Suisse* 2021: Bodily Encounters

168 Skirting The Center: Svetlana Kana Radević on the Periphery of Postwar Architecture

170 The Majlis

172 Tropicalia. Architecture, Materials, Innovative Systems

174 Without Land / Pomerium

176 Young European Architects

178 Young Talent Architecture Award 2020. Educating together

180 Index of participants

Participating
Countries

Neighbouring apartments. Conceptual model of the pavilion *In Our Home*.
Courtesy and © curatorial team of *In Our Home*

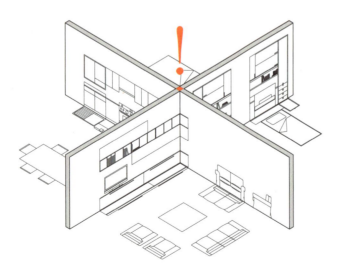

Pavilion concept, scheme 1.
Courtesy and © curatorial team of *In Our Home*

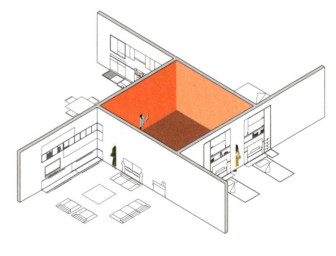

Pavilion concept, scheme 2.
Courtesy and © curatorial team of *In Our Home*

Albania

IN OUR HOME

We share a wall – yet, we don't know each other's names. At the dawn of a new decade, the answer to the question of how we will live together could be simple: know your neighbour!

A special spontaneous bond, owing only to the immediate proximity offered by our living spaces. It depends on each and everyone's willingness to communicate with a stranger. Not just any stranger, but a stranger who has a lot in common with us, who lives just a few metres away. Together with these strangers, we shape the identity of our apartment building, our neighbourhood, our city.

Depending on this bond, our perception of life in our home, in our building and neighbourhood might completely change – it might be negative and alienating, but it might also be positively meaningful.

In Albania, less than 20 years ago next-door neighbours were often closer than relatives. These neighbours were the people we shared our morning coffee with, the people we asked to borrow an extra chair from for a special dinner, the people we trusted with our house key when we were away, the kids we played with outside, the people who let us use their phone when we didn't have one.

Today, diving deep into the waters of globalization, we too have moved toward an isolated indifference. The questions we should first ask ourselves are, 'How many neighbours did our grandparents know?' 'How many neighbours did our parents know?' 'And how many neighbours do we know?'

Convinced that the quality of our life together depends on our collective consciousness about this bond, the Albanian pavilion attempts to symbolically bring to our attention what or who may lie beyond our apartment walls.

It is an invitation to cross these thin barriers and discover the gift of a connection that fulfils our need to *belong* and makes a *place* out of our address, transforming our *building*, our *neighbourhood*, and even our *city* into something much more meaningful.

Three neighbouring *apart*ments, besides sharing walls, secretly share a space that can only come to life if the neighbours are willing to make the discovery.

Commissioner
Elva Margariti,
Minister of Culture
of the Republic of Albania

Curators and Participants
Fiona Mali
Irola Andoni
Malvina Ferra
Rudina Breçani

Coordinators
Doris Alimerko
Sonila Kora

In Collaboration with
The Central State Film
Archives

With the Support of
Municipality of Tirana

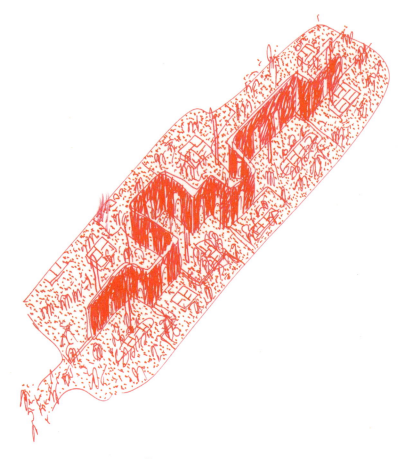

All images: *La casa infinita*, 2020

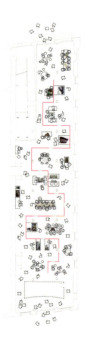

Argentina

LA CASA INFINITA

You cannot enter *La casa infinita* (The infinite house); you are always inside of it. It is so large that you cannot leave. It is open and wide, simple and discreet. It does not have a predetermined path.

We believe that each of us lives in a different house, but in the end we realise that it is always the same. We share it. It belongs to everyone.

The house is so large that you can go around it on foot, by bike, car, train, bus, or even by plane. It has big gardens, with mountains and prairies. It has small rooms, with beds and tables. Every space is connected. Going around the house becomes a lifelong journey.

La casa infinita represents our world, the world we inhabit together.

Visitors to the pavilion will find a series of undefined spaces wriggling along a wall that articulates and connects them. This wall derives from the geometric manipulation of the traditional Argentine family house. The pink of the wall suggests the usual technique applied in our country – a mixture of bull's blood and lime.

Each visitor experiences as many houses as paths taken, just as we do in our everyday lives.

A representative selection of works and plans by housing projects is exhibited. All these were built in Argentina as a result of private and public initiatives, contests and investments, through official and private financing. The house is furnished with tables and beds on which the chosen pieces are displayed, making use of blueprints, photographs, drawings, and miniatures.

The pavilion's curatorship intends to highlight those projects in which common areas are fundamental to the way we relate to each other, and the way we choose to live together.
—GERARDO CABALLERO

Commissioner
Juan Falú

Curator
Gerardo Caballero

Deputy Curator
Paola Gallino

Work Team
Paola Gallino
Franco Brachetta
Sebastián Flosi
Leonardo Rota
Ana Babaya
Sofía Rothman
Emmanuel Leggeri
Gerardo Bordi
Edgardo Torres

Elevation of the interactive architectural installation at the grounds
of Palazzo Ca' Zenobio

Conceptual photocollage

Conceptual photocollage

Republic of Armenia

HYBRIDITY: A MACHINE FOR LIVING TOGETHER

In today's world of multifaceted cultures and relentless movement, we need to better understand how people develop a sense of identity and learn to coexist in varying places. The pavilion encourages visitors to explore the fundamentals of human interaction through a physical expression of the living process among a hybridity of identities.

Today, as we ask *How will we live together?*, we bear in mind that Armenia has a long history of tackling this question as a place of both gathering and separation. Throughout the diaspora, millions of Armenians have spread out all over the world and have adapted to new sociocultural contexts while enriching the existing ones. The pavilion tries to translate this human capacity to interact with each other and influence cultures both as individuals and as a community, in familiar as well as unusual spaces.

Hybridity: a Machine for Living Together is an interactive architectural installation emerging from the grounds of the Palazzo Ca' Zenobio and various locations in Armenia. It works similarly to how we, as humans, use our perceptions, senses, and social interactions to live with each other. Merging the digital and the physical – and occasionally making mistakes along the way – this fantastical architectural contraption attempts to generate new formulas, spaces, and experiences for living together in the never-ending process of learning and transformation.
—ALLEN SAYEGH

Commissioner
Tina Chakarian

Curator
Allen Sayegh
(Vosguerichian)

Participants
INVIVIA
Storaket Architectural Studio

Organiser
Araik Khzmalyan
(Deputy Minister of
    the Ministry of Education,
    Science, Culture and Sport
    of the Republic of Armenia)

Coordinator
Mariam Gigoyan

Communication
Lelag Vosguian

With the Support of
The Ministry of Education,
    Science, Culture and Sport
    of the Republic of Armenia
Harvard Graduate School
    of Design's Responsive
    Environments and Artifacts
    Lab (REAL Lab)

Pavilion of Australia. Image SJB Architects

Inbetween centrepiece. Image SJB Architects

Indigenous Languages map. Image SJB Architects

Australia

INBETWEEN

The project presents a series of architectural works from Australia and across the Pacific region that strengthen cultural understanding between non-indigenous and First Nations peoples. Projects that powerfully demonstrate the capacity of architecture to revive and enhance Indigenous voice, identity and culture.

Inviting our neighbours in. Australia is fortunate enough to be one of only 29 countries that have a pavilion, a fixed space within the Giardini in Venice. However, in a time where a more inclusive philosophy toward people and places is more necessary than ever, it seems only appropriate that the Pavilion be shared with our neighbours from the Pacific Region.

Like Australia, Polynesia (including Aotearoa New Zealand) Melanesia and Micronesia have dealt with the challenges of European occupation, settlement and colonisation. The impact of this occupation and modernisation continues to affect these regions. *Indigenous design and co-authorship.* The exhibition encourages a connection to our neighbours, a recognition of our neighbours, a sharing with our neighbours. It responds deeply to Hashim Sarkis's theme 'How will we live together?' by highlighting a series of works that authentically, and appropriately, demonstrate the protection, revival and celebration of Indigenous culture.

It looks at how we might better preserve and integrate Indigenous knowledge systems into architecture through processes of thinking and designing that lead to deeper, more layered outcomes. In parallel, it is also about providing a stage for more vulnerable, isolated or simply lesser-known islands, territories and atolls. The multiple effects of 'western' occupation, migration and climate degradation will one day see some of these unique populations on the brink of dislocation and irreversible cultural impact.

This Exhibition sees Australia inviting its neighbours from the Pacific to share the Pavilion, collectively present examples of architecture and importantly, the engagement processes behind the architecture that powerfully represent non-indigenous and Indigenous ideologies simultaneously. Architecture becomes the enabler to connect, to evoke Country, to reveal layers of history and memory, and to give cultural expression, predicated on a people-centred approach to a shared humanity.

Commissioner
Janet Holmes á Court

Curators
Tristan Wong
(SJB Architects) and
Jefa Greenaway
(Greenaway
Architects)

Participants
SJB Architects
Greenaway Architects
Architects without
   Frontiers
Baldasso Cortese
Cathy Kubany
Cox
Daniel Stricker
Edition Office
Gregory Burgess
   Architects
Gresley Abas
   Architects
Grimshaw
Lyons
Michael Mossman
NSW Government
   Architect's Office
Neeson Murcutt +
   Neille
Officer Woods
   Architects
Paul Herzich
Sibling Architecture
Susan Dugdale &
   Associates
Taylor + Hinds
   Architects
UniSA
University of Sydney
Vincent Heimann
Warren and Mahoney
Woods Bagot
the National University
   of Samoa

Organiser
The Royal Australian
   Institute of
   Architects (RAIA)

Creative Team
Elizabeth Grant
Aaron Puls,
Jordyn Milliken
Ash Parsons

The Royal Australian Institute of Architects (RAIA) recognises the significant contribution from Network Venice Sponsors and donors and the support given by the Australia Council for the Arts. The RAIA gratefully acknowledges the generous support from its key sponsors Brickworks and BEC. The Curators would also like to acknowledge the invaluable support and collaboration of Mosster Studio (Audio/Visual Creator), Institute for Advanced Architecture of Catalonia (Digital Fabrication), Studio Round with Maree Clarke (Branding, Graphic Design), Tony Birch (Poetry), Bluescope (Supplier), Big Plans (Prototype / Projection Testing), Fkd Studio (Prototyping/Virtual Reality), Arup (Building Services) and Perks and Mini (Merchandise)

Platform Urbanism – onstage/offstage, 2020.
© Centre for Global Architecture

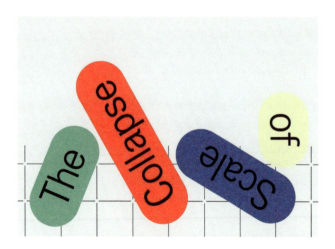

Platform Austria, slogan, Centre for Global Architecture, 2020.
Graphic Design: Bueronardin. © Platform Austria

Platform Austria, slogan, Centre for Global Architecture, 2020.
Graphic Design: Bueronardin. © Platform Austria

Austria

PLATFORM AUSTRIA

A phenomenon is haunting the world – the phenomenon of platform urbanism. Today, it is no longer architects, urban planners, politicians, and citizens who lead decision-making regarding the design of our future habitats. In their place we are seeing platform developers disrupting conventional forms of spatial production and taking on a global role as planning superpowers. They are radically reorganising access to a wide spectrum of fundamental domains, such as education, labour, transport, housing, health, and culture.

Platform Austria aims to challenge this new form of monopoly over the imagination of our future environments by transforming the pavilion itself into a platform. Responding to the recent experience of a technologically facilitated 'immobilisation' of societies and a concomitant rise of platform industries, we have invited more than fifty contributors from around the world to share their views on platform urbanism via an online blog.

In the Austrian pavilion, these blog contributions form part of two major installation pieces that highlight the interaction between economic and social forces in platform environments:

Access is the new capital – *The platform is my boyfriend*

As a forum of exchange, *Platform Austria* also includes:

– *The collapse of scale*: visual research into emerging typologies of platform urbanism produced by the Centre for Global Architecture

– *Data is a relation not a property*: public debates with guest speakers from around the world scheduled to take place at the pavilion on Saturday afternoons

– *We like*: an open-access online portal for sharing and commenting on images of architectures, cities, and environments we like: www.platform-austria.org

Platform Austria has a clear goal: to utilise the unique opportunity presented by the global reach of Biennale Architettura 2021 to generate a collaboratively formed study of the impact of platform urbanism on our cities, as well as to articulate alternative visions of an architecture we would like to see shaping our future – reclaiming public authority over the task at hand is key to formulating a truly democratic response to the question *How will we live together*?

Commissioner
Austrian Federal Ministry for Arts, Culture, the Civil Service and Sport – Division Arts and Culture

Curators
Peter Mörtenböck
Helge Mooshammer

Participants
Centre for Global Architecture, bloggers and guest discussants, including Ross Exo Adams, Tom Avermaete, Lucia Babina, Jochen Becker, Daniel Cardoso Llach, Ofri Cnaani, Teddy Cruz & Fonna Forman, Peggy Deamer, Sylvia Eckermann & Gerald Nestler, Fairwork Project, Pedro Gadanho, Benjamin Gerdes, Stephen Graham, Orit and Tal Halpern, Owen Hatherley, Gabu Heindl, Leo Hollis, Into the Black Box, Andreas Kofler, Bernadette Krejs & Andrea Börner, Maroš Krivy, Peter Lang, Mona Mahall & Asli Serbest, Jonathan Massey, metroZones, Sandro Mezzadra, Susan Moore & Scott Rodgers, Louis Moreno, Edgar Pieterse, João Prates Vital Ruivo, Heidi Pretterhofer, Vyjayanthi Rao, Saskia Sassen, Manuel Shvartzberg-Carrió, Slutty Urbanism, Douglas Spencer, Matthew Stewart, Ravi Sundaram, Tiziana Terranova, This Machine Kills, Ignacio Valero, Matias Viegener, Alan Wiig, and others

....

Curatorial Assistance
Carmen Lael Hines (Centre for Global Architecture)

Research Assistance
Christian Frieß
Lovro Koncar-Gamulin
Pieter de Cuyper
Ruth Köchl
Julius Bartz
(Centre for Global Architecture)

Exhibition Design Spatial Concept
Peter Mörtenböck
Helge Mooshammer

Design
mostlikely sudden workshop
Pretterhofer Arquitectos

Project and Production Management
section.a

Visual communication
Bueronardin

Online-Platform Programming
Philipp Daun

Video Production
RAUM.FILM

Structural Engineer
Bollinger + Grohmann

Support on site
M+B studio

With the Support of
Land Oberösterreich, FWF Der Wissenschaftsfond, TU Wien, BIG Bundesimmobilien-gesellschaft, Wien Holding, Zumtobel, Barta & Partner, Association of the Austrian Wood Industries, Triflex, BAI, Arnold Investments, Laufen, Österreichisches Siedlungswerk, PEFC, Aspern, VEH, Kvadrat, Bioweingut Lenikus, Bollinger + Grohmann, Geyer & Geyer, Weiss, Bellutti Planen, Adler, Rema, TEMA

Yakov Khalip, *Nagorno-Karabakh. Old Shusha view*, 1937.
Courtesy Lumiere Gallery, Moscow

Yakov Khalip, *Nagorno-Karabakh, A bridge in the mountains near Old Shusha* 1937.
Courtesy Lumiere Gallery, Moscow

Republic of Azerbaijan

BACK TO THE FUTURE

Commissioner
Mammad Ahmadzada,
   Ambassador of the Republic
   of Azerbaijan

Curator
Emin Mammadov

Participants
Yakov Khalip
Rashad Alakbarov
Nariman Memarlig -
   Architectural Studio

Executor
Heydar Aliyev Foundation
   (Baku)

Scientific Advisor
Eva Maria Auch

Coordinators
Narmina Khalilova
Farhad Boyukzada
Paolo De Grandis
Carlotta Scarpa
PDG Arte Communications

Finding the key to achieving harmonious coexistence among ethnic groups with different cultural traditions in a multiethnic state is a major challenge worldwide.

The year 2021 marks Azerbaijan's first participation in the 17th International Architecture Exhibition of La Biennale di Venezia, realised by the Heydar Aliyev Foundation. The Azerbaijan pavilion is proud to present *Back to the future*, an exhibition that draws attention to the phenomenon of the art of coexistence through the emotionally charged, refined, memory-laden photographs of Yakov Khalip, the fascinating shadow installations of Rashad Alakbarov (which exist only when illuminated and viewed from a particular vantage point, causing viewers to question their perception of reality), and the philosophy-respecting immemorial architectural heritage solutions proposed by the Nariman Memarlig Architectural Studio with the scientific approach of Eva Maria Auch, Humboldt University, Berlin, Germany.

Located at the crossroads of various civilizations, Azerbaijan, throughout the centuries, has become famous for its national cultural diversity. Representatives of various nationalities and faiths live in an atmosphere of peace, welfare, mutual understanding, and dialogue. Our people's tolerant way of life also finds expression in the full range of literary, artistic, scientific, philosophical, political, and legal works and documents created through the ages by the Azerbaijani people, which are a testament to their rich multicultural collective past. The experience of Azerbaijan shows that respect and equality are the fundamental principles for maintaining friendly relationships between cultures and nationalities.

The oil boom at the end of the nineteenth century enabled the commissioning of great architectural monuments by major world-renowned architects, whose creations in that golden age still grace the city of Baku.

In more recent years, since independence from the Soviet Union, this tradition has been revived and extended with invitations to such eminent architects as Zaha Hadid and COOP Himmelb(l)au, to name but two, nurturing the next generation of modern architecture. On the strength of this legacy and looking to the future, Azerbaijan is determined to pursue this successful creative path, breathing new life into the once illustrious city of Shusha, welcoming and resettling the full diversity of its cultural minorities, and restoring its great historic status once again.

Multicultural, multilinguistic, multi-traditional – living side by side.
—EMIN MAMMADOV

Pearling Path Visitors Centre. Project by Valerio Olgiati, Muharraq, 2019.
Photo Olgiati Archive

Internal facade of Al Jalahma House, Muharraq, 2016.
Photo Camille Zakharia

Pearling Path public squares. Project by Bureau
Bas Smets and OFFICE Kersten Geers David
Van Severen, Muharraq, 2014. Photo Bas Princen

Kingdom of Bahrain

IN MUHARRAQ: THE PEARLING PATH

For millennia, pearling and its associated trades shaped the economy and culture of Bahrain and led to the flourishing of one of its main cities, Muharraq, in the mid-nineteenth century. Pearls built Muharraq. Financed by the sale of pearls that were extracted from oysters, the city's structures were built out of the coral stone that housed these same oysters, its culture and social life derived from the rhythm of pearling activities. The city evolved in close synergy with its natural context and resources.

As the pearl industry declined due to irreversible economic changes in the early twentieth century, the city fell into neglect, losing its close relationship with the sea, especially following extensive reclamation of its coast.

Today, the surviving traces of Muharraq's tangible and intangible pearling heritage are rare testimonies to the Gulf's transregional socioeconomic connections before the discovery of oil. However, in comparison to other historical cities and apart from the urban footprint of the city and its network of streets, little architectural heritage remains and the social fabric of the city has changed.

In 2005, the first conservation initiatives were launched and over the last 15 years they have grown to encompass an urban regeneration project, the UNESCO World Heritage-listed Pearling, Testimony of an Island Economy project, which includes the conservation of sixteen listed historic properties related to the pearling economy, two visitor centres, sixteen public spaces, four multi-storey parking areas, a pedestrian bridge, a beach, and three oyster beds. The project is a work in progress that is constantly adapting itself to the challenges of a changing city.

The exhibition presents both the results and the process of making, through models, objects, minutes of meetings, artefacts, drawings, and conversations, showing the project in its current state. It explores the challenges in reviving the memory of pearling, as a backdrop to a culturally-led development approach and as a binder between the physical makings of the city and its identity. It also raises the question of how to create public space in segregated societies, whether it's still possible and appropriate to build monuments today, if there isn't a more sustainable way of using our resources. In short, it questions whether pearls, oysters, coral stones, cars, and humans can sustainably and generously cohabit in the city today.

Commissioner
Mai bint Mohammed Al Khalifa, President of the Bahrain Authority for Culture & Antiquities

Curators
Noura Al Sayeh-Holtrop
Ghassan Chemali

Participants
Bureau Bas Smets
Christian Kerez
OFFICE Kersten Geers David Van Severen
Pearling Path Team
Fatema Abdali Abdulnabi
Shatha Abu El Fath
Ahmad Abd El Nabi
Batool Al Shaikh
Mario Affaki
Fatema Al Hayki
Ahmad Al Jishi
Mustafa Al Zurki
Ronan Dayot
Wissam Fadlalah
Sarah Fareed Hassani
Lucia Gomez
Yehya Hassan
Marwa Nabeel
Tamer Nassar
Faisal Soudaga
Shadi Taha
Studio Anne Holtrop
Studio Gionata Rizzi
Valerio Olgiati

Assistant Curator
Batool Al Shaikh

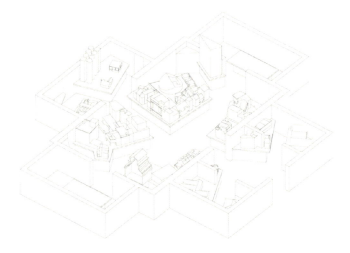

Composite Presence, 2020.
All images © Bovenbouw Architectuur

Belgium

COMPOSITE PRESENCE

How do city and architecture flourish together? This question is central to this three-dimensional 'capriccio' that displays a fictional yet recognisable urban Flemish environment.

Over time, the informal city in Flanders and Brussels has developed a unique relationship with its architecture. This staged urban landscape reveals how historical layers, morphological peculiarities, and unforeseen collisions are an endless source of energy for contemporary architectural production. The diverse selection of works also brings out a certain thematic discipline when it comes to the production of an attractive urban environment. The interface between the public domain and the building, the plasticity of the street, the joyful reuse of the existing fabric, the elegant scale jump... all these issues have gradually become key components of the collective discourse on how to produce a lasting environment.

The model landscape simultaneously depicts the potential of a phenomenological approach to composing a cityscape. Away from the technological, ideological and historical debates that dominated twentieth-century conceptions of the city, this capriccio expresses a strong belief in the fruitful co-existence of lively differences.

The question *how to live together* addresses the world of the designer. How does one building contribute to the success of a shared cityscape? And how do issues like composition, material culture, memory, and diversity create an advanced built environment?

Fifty recent projects by forty-five contemporary Belgian practices contribute to the imaginary landscape. This selection of projects depicts a healthy architectural ecology in which different styles, functions, and typologies coincide. Many of these projects are refurbishments and adaptations, adding up to the variegated experience of form, time, and texture. Whether projects are modest reuses or shiny newbies, they all share an interest in contributing to a city that is simultaneously patched up and balanced.

The project selection also reveals the importance of the current policies in Belgium when it comes to city planning and tendering. Many of the designs in this cityscape stem from procedures set up by city architects, the Flemish Government Architect, and related committees and administrations. This model arrangement simulates the negotiated urban environment that has slowly emerged from this field of expertise.

—DIRK SOMERS

Commissioner
Flanders Architecture
    Institute

Curator
Bovenbouw
    Architectuur

Participants
360 Architecten,
Architecten Broekx-
Schiepers, architecten
de vylder vinck
taillieu, architecten
Els Claessens en Tania
Vandenbussche,
Architectenbureau
Bart Dehaene, Arjaan
De Feyter Interior
Architects, Baeten
Hylebos Architecten,
BLAF architecten,
Bovenbouw
Architectuur, BULK
architecten, Collectief
Noord Architecten,
COUSSÉE & GORIS
architecten,
De Smet Vermeulen
architecten,
Dhooge & Meganck
Architectuur,
Dierendonckblancke
architecten,
DMT architecten,
dmvA, Eagles of
Architecture,
FELT architecture
& design, Frederic
Vandoninck Wouter
Willems architecten
in collaboration
with Dennis Tyfus,
GRAUX & BAEYENS
architecten, HUB,
Marie-José Van Hee
architecten, META
architectuurbureau,
murmuur architecten,
OFFICE Kersten Geers

David Van Severen,
ono architectuur,
Poot Architectuur,
PULS architecten,
RAAMWERK,
Robbrecht en Daem &
Dierendonckblancke
in collaboration with
VK & Arup, Schenk
Hattori Architecture
Atelier, Stéphane
Beel Architects,
STUDIOLO
architectuur in
collaboration with
Koen Matthys, tim
peeters architecten,
Tim Rogge
Architectuur Studio,
Tom Thys architecten,
TRANS architectuur
stedenbouw, AgwA
in collaboration with
Ferrière Architectes,
URA Yves Malysse
Kiki Verbeeck,
VAN GELDER
TILLEMAN
architecten,
Vermeiren – De
Coster Architecten,
VERS.A
ARCHITECTURE

With the Support of
The Flemish
    Government

Gustavo Minas, photographic essay on Brasilia Bus Station
(architecture by Lucio Costa), 2015

Luiza Baldan, photographic essay
on Pedregulho Residential Building
(architecture by Affonso Eduardo Reidy), 2009

Joana França, photographic documentation on Brasilia Bus Station
(architecture by Lucio Costa), 2010

Brazil

UTOPIAS OF COMMON LIFE

Commissioner
José Olympio da Veiga Pereira,
  Fundação Bienal de São
  Paulo

Curators
Alexandre Brasil
André Luiz Prado
Bruno Santa Cecilia
Carlos Alberto Maciel
Henrique Penha
Paula Zasnicoff

Participants
Aiano Bemfica, Cris Araújo,
  Edinho Vieira
Alexandre Delijaicov | Grupo
  de Pesquisa Metrópole
  Fluvial – Faculdade de
  Arquitetura e Urbanismo da
  Universidade de São Paulo
Amir Admoni
Gustavo Minas
Joana França
Leonardo Finotti
Luiza Baldan

Organisers
Fundação Bienal de São Paulo;
Ministry of Foreign Affairs –
  Embassy of Brazil in Rome;
Ministry of Tourism – Special
  Secretary of Culture

Brazil's oldest manifestation of the idea of utopia is *ivy marã ei*. More than 5,000 years ago, the Guarani people used to wander around the territory in the search of a 'Land without Affliction', a place that would be a mirror of the Earth, but without hunger, war, and disease.

Modern Brazilian architecture was driven by the values of amplifying the public realm, welcoming differences, reducing inequalities, and preparing the territory to offer open platforms to foster full coexistence in all its complexity, without sublimating its contradictions. These values, present in contemporary initiatives, stimulated the imagination of 'other places' – utopias – for common life.

Past Futures portrays a moment when the belief that Brazil was the 'country of the future' still existed and everything was yet to be built. Two photo essays reveal the strength and deviations of recent daily appropriation in two works that, at the time, were exemplary in transforming the ideals of modernity: the Pedregulho Residential Complex (1947) in Rio de Janeiro and the Brasilia Bus Station Platform (1957).

Nowadays, designing new buildings is no longer the country's crucial pressing need. Rethinking existing infrastructures, giving them different functionalities with a collective-oriented design, and renovating countless abandoned buildings in central areas are emerging challenges. *Present Futures* introduces two specially commissioned films that reflect on the possibility of reversing the main problems of large Brazilian cities, imagining a re-signified life through the transformation of housing and mobility infrastructures. These two pieces operate on the existing, not in 'another place', by reversing the logic of exclusion imposed by the dichotomy between center and periphery. Through suggesting a reconciliation with nature, they throw light on new possibilities for a richer, more diverse, qualified and transformative coexistence, less unequal, more friendly, and environmentally conscious way of life.

Impostor Cities, Pavilion of Canada Videodrome, 2019

MR. X, Dundas Street Toronto, Shape of Water, 2017

Canada

IMPOSTOR CITIES

Canada's architecture is film-famous. However, unlike Berlin or Rio de Janeiro, our cities rarely play themselves in film and television. Toronto stands in for Tokyo. Vancouver and Montreal masquerade as Moscow, Paris, and New York.

Impostor Cities celebrates the legacy of over a half-century of Canada's most renowned architectural doubles. It introduces a playful yet pointed counterproposition to the popular image of our national identity by investigating why Canada's buildings are so good at doubling as elsewhere. How do we think about authenticity and identity in an age where artifice in media is indistinguishable from reality?

In his book *Amérique* (1986), French sociologist Jean Baudrillard describes the North American city as 'a screen of signs and formulas'. He writes that the North American city 'seems to have stepped out of the movies. To grasp its secrets, you should not, then, begin with the city and move towards the screen; you should begin with the screen and move towards the city'. In response, *Impostor Cities* imagines architecture in new modes of consumption and appreciation.

The exterior of the pavilion, wrapped in green fabric, draws attention amidst the excitement of the 17th International Architecture Exhibition, highlighting the controversial symbolism of the pavilion's 'tepee-shaped' architecture. Through CGI technology, an iconic Canadian building takes the pavilion's place in the Giardini, transforming a historic part of Venice into Canada. Inside, a multiscreen video installation and a library of impostor buildings explore how fictional worlds rely on our real cities. It puts visitors in movie mode, inducing new perceptions of Canadian architecture through film.

Impostor Cities expands uncanny moments: new recognition of the Canadian pavilion and the shock of recognition of familiar cityscapes and buildings onscreen. The exhibition highlights the role Canadian architecture has quietly played in shaping the world's cultural narratives through film.

Commissioner
Canada Council for
    the Arts

Curator
David Theodore

Participant
T B A / Thomas
    Balaban Architect

Project Manager
Thomas Balaban

Project Designer
Jennifer Thorogood

Graphic Designer
Pawel Karwowski

Sound Curation
and Design
Randolph Jordan

Project Research
+ Design Team
Nick Cabelli
Cameron Cummings
Mikaèle Fol
Joel Friesen
François-Mathieu
    Mariaud de Serre

Film Editor
John Gurdebeke

Audiovisual Integration
Éric Fauque

Surround Concept
and Mixing
Florian Grond

Interactive Design
Team
Jane Kate Wong
Eva Peng
Wipawe Sirikolkarn
X Y Feng

Project Logistics
Tamara
    Andruszkiewicz

With the Support of
SAJO
McGill University
Université de Montréal
Panasonic
Ontario Association
    of Architects
frog
MR. X
Atelier Zébulon
Perron

Portrait of Guillermo Lazo.
Photo Paloma Montecinos Ochoa

Portrait of Antonella Aros and Jordana Carreño.
Photo Paloma Montecinos Ochoa

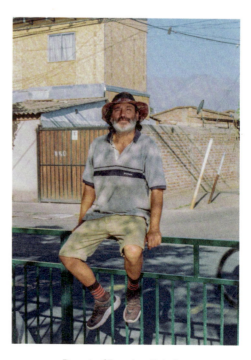

Portrait of Francisco Faúndez.
Photo Paloma Montecinos Ochoa

Chile

TESTIMONIAL SPACES

The main piece in the Chilean pavilion at the 17th International Architecture Exhibition is 500 testimonies transformed into 500 paintings. Based on a set of formal rules and collective work where authorship is diluted within the community, painters and historians have brought together the stories of the emblematic José María Caro settlement and turned them into images. These latter go through different spaces, recalling past and present lives within this community.

The question *How will we live together?* implies a reflection on the experiences of how we have lived as a community, the different historical and political cycles that are part of the territory we inhabit, and how memory allows us to look at our past and hence put forward a joint view.

The José María Caro settlement is located south of the central peripheral beltway of Santiago in Chile and is part of a carefully planned social integration process. In the late 1950s and early 1960s, the government's Housing Corporation Office implemented a new housing plan that would bring different social classes together within the same territory. The territory would include informal settlements for freelance or middle-class workers, members of the armed forces and government employees in eight distinct sectors organised along the railway that connects the country's central region to the south.

Testimonial Spaces is an exhibition that focuses on pursuing memories, yearnings, and the spatial tactics of an integrated life; on a city that is the end result of an inventory filled with stereotypes; on a biographical city where architectures, imaginary routines, and common spaces and circumstances rebuild an already inhabited and imperfect city, longed for and idealised: a house, a park, a street-market, a sports area, the neighbourhood, the fact of living next to each other.

Commissioner
Cristóbal Molina,
    Ministry of Cultures, Arts
    and Heritage of Chile

Curators
Emilio Marín
Rodrigo Sepúlveda

Direction of Contents
Pablo Ferrer
Emilio Marín
Rodrigo Sepúlveda

Pavilion Design
Emilio Marín
Rodrigo Sepúlveda
Alessandra Dal Mos

Historian
Juan Radic

Graphic Identity
María Gracia Fernández

Museography
Pablo Brugnoli

Lighting Consultancy
Victoria Campino

Organiser
Ministry of Cultures,
    Arts and Heritage of Chile

With the Support of
Direction of Cultural Affairs
    (DIRAC) of the Ministry
    of Foreign Affairs of Chile

Together we heal, 2020.
Render Atelier TeamMinus

Snow in the Forbidden City, 2020.
Courtesy and © The Palace Museum

Together we learn (Part I), 2020.
Render Atelier TeamMinus

Together we learn (Part II), 2020.
Render Atelier TeamMinus

Together we feel: hear the yuan-er, 2020.
Render Atelier TeamMinus

People's Republic of China

YUAN-ER, A COURTYARD-OLOGY: FROM THE MEGA TO THE MICRO

The theme of the 17th International Architecture Exhibition asks how architecture may contribute to equality, connectivity, and unity. This brings us to a familiar typology: *yuan-er*, which in Chinese is a multifamily courtyard, and refers both to the physical space and the people who inhabit it. The courtyard has constituted a vibrant co-living typology across cultures and across time. *Yuan-er* has also constituted the base molecule for all traditional urban and social fabrics in China, with examples ranging from the mega, such as the Forbidden City, to the micro, such as the *hutong*. Not only has *yuan-er* been the bearer of ideas from the past, but it also continues to inspire architects and artists who are searching for hints of the future.

The Chinese pavilion poses a question regarding *yuan-er*. How was it able, and how is it still able, to bring such diverse people so close together? What are the space–body relations that generate cohesive urban communities extending from one *yuan-er* to another? How could the wisdom of past *yuan-er* benefit the architecture of our time for people living together, online as well as offline?

The pavilion has five sections. In section 1, *Together we learn (Part I)*, various architects practising in China are invited to give individual stories of inspiration and interventions related to *yuan-er* through videos played on tablets and phones. In section 2, *Together we learn (Part II)*, six Chinese architects and six historians dissect classic cases and give radical contemporary interpretations through hologram projections. In section 3, *Together we design*, visitors are invited to design their own *yuan-er*, using the engine designed by an AI artist featuring the vocabulary of six young Chinese architects. In section 4, *Together we feel: hear the yuan-er,* an artist's sound installation takes the visitors on a journey of senses through the *yuan-er*. In section 5, *Together we heal*, the parlour in a real *yuan-er* (the garden) outside the pavilion provides stories of life together (both off- and online) through the Coronavirus epidemic.

Commissioner
China Arts and
    Entertainment
    Group Ltd.
    (CAEG)

Curator
Zhang Li

Participants
Zhu Zheqin
    (Dadawa)
He Wanyu
Cui Kai
Chang Qing
Zhuang Weimin
Zhou Kai
Liu Jiakun
Xiao Wei & Cadi
Lyu Zhou
Liu Chang
Zhao Peng
Michele Bonino &
    PoliTo
Chen Xiong
Cui Tong
Dong Gong
Gui Xuewen
Guo Mingzhuo
Hu Yue
Li Cundong
Li Hu & Huang
    Wenjing
Li Xinggang
Liu Doreen Heng
Liu Xiaodu
Liu Yichun & Chen
    Yifeng
Loehlein, Gisela &
    Xjtlu
Lyu Pinjing; Ma
    Yansong
Mei Hongyuan
Meng Yan
Ni Yang
Qi Xin
Shen Di
Shen Zuowei
Song Zhaoqing
Sun Yimin

Wang Hui
Wang Xiao'an
Yang Ying
Zhang Jie
Zhang Ming
Zhang Pengju
Zhang Tong
Zhang Yue
Zhao Yang
Zhao Yuanchao
Zhu Xiaodi
and many others

....

**Curators
Assistants**
Ye Yang
Bai Xue
Deng Huishu
Marta Mancini

Research Team
School of
    Architecture,
    Tsinghua University
    / Department
    of Architectural
    Heritage, The Palace
    Museum / Silk Road
    Artistic Research and
    Collaboration and
    Innovation Center,
    Central Academy
    of Fine Arts /
    World Architecture
    Magazine
    Publications

Producer
Wang Chen

Artistic Advisors
Wu Hongliang
Yue Jieqiong
Zhao Peng

**Display Design
and Graphic
Design**
Atelier TeamMinus

Organiser
Ministry of Culture
    and Tourism
    of the People's
    Republic of
    China

Presented by
China International
    Exhibition
    Agency

With the Support of
The Palace
    Museum
Beijing OLP Public
    Design Company
Hongri Lighting

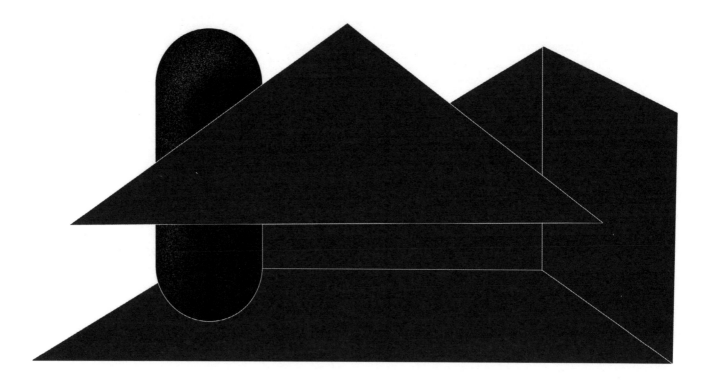

Togetherness/Togetherless

Croatia

TOGETHERNESS/ TOGETHERLESS

Being together refers to the use of a unique space and time by two or more people who are in a communicative relationship. This state of being together is the precondition for sensory and intellectual stimuli that we experience individually or in a group. In the dynamic relationship between individuals and their environment, which is, for most of us, made up primarily of other people, not only is a community created but we, as individuals, are also created.

One of the key questions is to understand where we can find this relationship, in which space and time. The answer to that question shapes our understanding of the world, the individual, community, and society. Technological possibilities give us the power to shape space and time at will, to accommodate individuals whose company we want and leave others outside. That way, the world in which we create ourselves resembles a film set or theatrical stage rather than a room or a city. Instead of real life, we live the scenes.

One of the symptoms of this condition is the marked iconophile present in our civilization, in which we affirm ourselves, individually or collectively, throughout an uninterrupted flow of images. Of course, this bending of space and time has its costs – economic, environmental, social, and political. Nevertheless, the awareness of those costs mostly ends up as representation, without any impact on the underlying structures.

The *Togetherness/Togetherless* exhibition is a composition of elements taken from the city in which people reside. A stage has been created where we can confirm our vision of any city tailored according to our preferences.

The pavilion is merely a basis for the dissemination and manipulation of images that will confirm their existence only in relation to other images. The elements used to create a spatial composition in the flow of exhibition areas in the Arsenale, suggesting a sense of being on a film set.

Commissioner
Ministry of Culture of the
Republic of Croatia

Curator
Idis Turato

Participants
Davor Mišković
Ida Križaj Leko
Ivan Dorotić
Leo Kirinčić
Maša Poljanec
Renato Stanković
Morana Matković
Jana Horvat

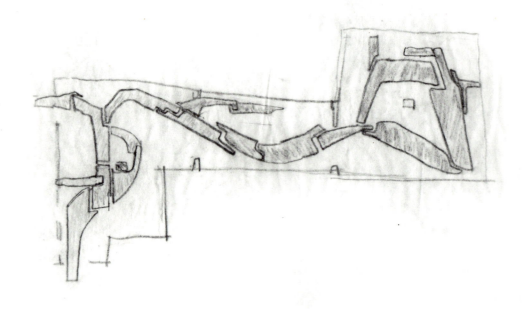

Sketch for 'Anachoresis' by Nasios Varnavas
(Urban Radicals)

Image sourced from the Archive of the Cyprus
Handicraft Centre

Research image from the Cyprus Pavilion Archive, 2021

Republic of Cyprus

ANACHORESIS UPON INHABITING DISTANCES

'Living-Together, especially idiorrhythmic Living-Together, implies an ethics (or a physics) of distance between cohabiting subjects.'
—Roland Barthes, *How To Live Together*

Commissioner
Petros Dymiotis

Curators
Era Savvides
Nasios Varnavas
(Urban Radicals)
Marina
   Christodoulidou
Evagoras Vanezis

Participant
Urban Radicals

....

**Deputy
Commissioner**
Angela Skordi

Dance-as-design
Georgia Tegou
Michalis Theophanous

Sound
Yiannis Christofides

Contributors
Serhan Ahmet-Tekbas
Thanasis Ikonomou
Eleonora Antoniadou
Nayia Savva
Veronika Antoniou
Teresa Tourvas
Mariza Daouti
Eftychios Savvidis
Rania Francis
Gergana Popova
Eleni Diana Elia
Kleanthis Roussos
Emilio Koutsoftides
Gabor Stark
Christophoros
   Kyriakides
Orestis Kyriakides
Kleanthis Kyriakou
Regner Ramos
Charis Nika
Sebastian Koukkides
Dakis Panayiotou
Theodoulos Polyviou

Natalie Savva
Mark Rist

Graphic Design
Studio Lin

Fabrication
Design & Making

Co-organisers
Ministry of Education,
   Culture, Youth and
   Sports
Cyprus Architects
   Association

What experiences can occur and what is the vocabulary that emerges when we explore the space within voluntary or enforced distances? 'Anachoresis' is a notion explicated by Roland Barthes as a metaphor for a life that entails an idiosyncratic template for the negotiation of distances and rhythms necessary for living together. Its foundational act is an abrupt jolt of departure, often leading to improvised retreats, which can either be solitary or cohabited. This improvisation manifests in unanticipated practices and spatial configurations and becomes a starting point for the architectural gesture of the Cyprus pavilion.

The gesture aims to distil the abruptness of the departure by proposing a quasi-monumental scaling up of the most social object and unifying agent of the domestic landscape, the table. The table shapes and is shaped by the pavilion's former domestic typology and the design inspires a metaphorical meander through the city. Its architecture suggests a micro-urbanism of co-operation and gathers contributions which re-envision spaces and social environments through the lens of collectivity, the inside and the outside, queerness, game, architectural traditions, technology, and virtual space.

Movement and sound are proposed as design tools that negotiate rhythm and idiorrhythmy. The resulting spaces generated by the gesture, movement, and sound agglomerate diverse characters into one entity of cohabitation while celebrating moments of tension between them. The (diverse) objects and functions suggest unplanned and improvised social, political, and material protocols of collectivity.

Do we long for the city to enter our domestic spaces and re-configure the scale upwards and outwards, so that another urban dimension can emerge and new localities can take place? Or do we, rather, long for an opportunity to reintroduce our domestic environments, our intimate micro-scales, into our cities, making public space more intimate and human? By catalysing new socialites to gather and develop, anachoresis nurtures the act of inhabiting the distances that may shape our collective experiences and the future of living together.

Water connects all life on earth. Throughout the pavilion, visitors can sense water in different stages and atmospheres;
as it enters, runs through and flows out of the exhibition. By opening ourselves up to the sensory experiences of our connectedness
with our surroundings, we also increase our ability to connect with each other. © Photo Hampus Berndtson

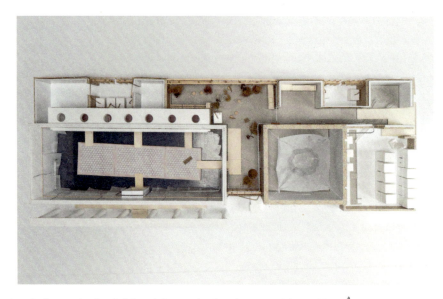

In the months ahead of the exhibition, ideas have been tested thoroughly in a 1:20 scale model
of the Danish Pavilion. © Photo Lundgaard & Tranberg Architects

The con-nect-ed-ness exhibition in the Danish
Pavilion is an architectural transformation of
the existing spaces. In one of the halls, visitors will
experience a suspended canvas sheet hanging
from the ceiling. It is part of the exhibition's water
cycle and reacts with the weather conditions
of Venice. © Photo Hampus Berndtson

Denmark

CON-NECT-ED-NESS

Commissioner
Kent Martinussen,
    The Danish Architecture
    Center

Curator
Marianne Krogh

Participants
Lundgaard & Tranberg
    Architects

Deputy Commissioner
Eva Kirstine Fabricius
(Danish Architecture Center)

Curator's Team
Jakob Rabe Petersen;
Olivia Viktoria Toftum;
Claudia Rebecca Juul
    Kassentoft;
Catherine Lyager Langer

Design Team
Lene Tranberg
Erik Frandsen
Benjamin Ter-Boch
Julius Nielsen
Henrik Schmidt
Signe Baadsgaard
Mikkel Kjærgård Christiansen
Artist Finn Reinbothe

Exhibition Installation
M+B studio
Fokdal Fountain

With the Support of
Ministry of Culture Denmark,
    Realdania
The Danish Arts Foundation

We live in a time when nature is perceived as something inherently different from ourselves. We have built societies, languages and ways of living that preclude us from sensing things any differently. Sensing that we too are nature, that we are connected. That is why we now need to invent new ways of inhabiting the earth.

Through the exhibition *con-nect-ed-ness* we ask ourselves how architecture can help us cultivate a holistic understanding and develop a new, meaningful relationship with the world as a place where humanity recognizes that everything is part of a larger whole: a single living system.

All life depends on water. Water exists everywhere on the planet in a dynamic cycle that the exhibition *con-nect-ed-ness* links to. Water harvested from the roof of the pavilion is made visible and tangible, it flows through the exhibition – who knows where it has been before and where it will go next? Who knows what other bodies, countries and centuries it has passed through? The cyclical flow and immanent boundlessness of water tie past, present and future together and preclude any possibility of isolating ourselves from each other, acknowledging that we are connected. The water carries time, disaster, life, the others. It flows through our shared spaces.

con-nect-ed-ness is a shared space: water is invited in, sensed and then flows out of the pavilion again. Through living bodies, evaporation, photosynthesis and percolation, people and water engage in a mutual process of becoming. Becoming is the nature of nature and nature always comes first. Nature is energy, rhythm, balance. When we create, we can allow these phenomena to enable a direct experience of our relationship with nature. Here lies a potential for a new world view that not only assigns value based on economic growth but sees wealth in variation, (bio)diversity and connectedness.

LiLeón, *Conexión.* Exhibition view

Conexión. Detail of the installation

Tobacco harvest

Dominican Republic

CONEXIÓN

Commissioner
Carmen Heredia de Guerrero,
   Minister of Culture of the
   Dominican Republic

Curator
Roberta Semeraro

Participants
Lidia León Cabral
and Alex Martínez Suárez
Jesús D'Alessandro
Juan Miguel Pérez
Julia Vicioso,
Orisell Medina-Lagrange
Traza_do (Collective of
   architects Melisa Vargas,
   Rafael Selman, Dante
   Luna, Javier Pérez, José
   Marion-Landais Alejandro
   Marranzini,Carlos Aguilar,
   Keith Thomas, Laura
   Troncoso, Liza Ortega,
   Santiago Camarena, Yaqui
   Núñez)
Michelle Valdez
Shaney Peña Gómez
Mizoocky Mota
Yomayra Martinó
Carmen Ortega
Ching Ling Ho
Sara Hermann
Virginia Flores-Sasso
Elia Mariel Martínez
Lissette Gil
Romina Santroni
Maribel Villalona

**On site Representative
for the Commissioner**
Iris Peynado

Organisation
Ministry of Culture of the
   Dominican Republic
LiLeón Foundation
Cultural Association
   RO.SA.M.

The project created by LiLeón for is a concrete example of architecture that supports and encourages a state of coexistence between individuals inside the space. It's no coincidence that the Anglican church is a pluralistic one, where diverse theological tendencies come together in harmony. Coexistence, understood as the connections between human beings, is a fundamental theme for LiLeón: 'Discovering the interconnections between science, nature, and spirituality, revealing the link between the intangible and the visible. My work reiterates the awareness of feeling that I am a reflection of a collective reality broader than personal individual reality. It reveals that we are all interconnected like drops from the same Ocean...'

The architect's focus on the Wabi Sabi concept of beauty in decay led her to design a kind of garden in which falling leaves cover the ground in a golden blanket and others drift upwards towards the vault. The modular and longitudinal arrangement of the panels is linked to the structure of the nave, echoing the placement of the stained-glass windows dedicated to famous English residents of Venice – including John Ruskin, who was the first to develop a theory of beauty in decay as applied to architecture.

The design, realised on semi-transparent panels, is made from fragments of tobacco leaves left there to dry, linking the work to the landscape of the Caribbean and its tobacco plantations.

During the year of the pandemic, Conexión has turned into an interdisciplinary platform featuring the participation of diverse professionals, all contributing their perspective to the world of architecture, design, and planning in response to the question 'How will we live together?'

Conexión can be considered a real example of living and inclusive architecture on a human scale, in which virtual and physical spaces complement one another in a shared experience of thinking together. Visitors equipped with digital devices will have the opportunity to connect remotely with the activities held in the Dominican Republic, and vice versa – the Dominican audience will also be able to participate via streaming in the events taking place inside the Pavilion in Venice.

—ROBERTA SEMERARO

The Blessed Fragments

Egypt

THE BLESSED FRAGMENTS

Hey you, hello,

it's me. Come on. Can't you see? Come closer. Look at me? No, no... come even closer. It is not my appearance you see; it is not the way I look. Come on, discover the origin of joy through the wrinkles on my face. Go deep and meditate on what lies hidden inside of me. Can you see now my real beauty mixed inside my humble fragments? If so, now you can see me. Sometimes they call me one of the poor people. Sometimes they call me one of the community scums. Actually, I am the black and white, the positive and negative. You need me to complete your world. I am the one who contains the peaceful balance that everyone needs to sustain this life; the one who sells you fresh bread every day with a humble smile. I am the one that everyone needs in this life.

I am the one in all and the all in one.

Before you go, please, put together my humble fragments considering me; my real inner value. Let me reveal my peaceful inner balance while spreading the blessed bread among people. Let me integrate with all people who need to live – together – a better life. Ask the planners, politicians, and decision-makers to consider me in their future strategies. Not only me, ask them to consider all of us; we are – the common people – those who do vital essential humble jobs in local communities. Inform them we do not need a designer to rearrange us. We do not need a clever clogs to re-format us simply because we are different in culture, habits, and the way we live. They may call us problems, fragments, an obstacle to development and progress, or people who are holding up the upgrading of coexistence with global communities. Yes, we are many. We are different. We are random, but we are not obstacles. We are positive potentials for a better future. Together, we are one. Our unity is in our humble diversity. We are unity without uniformity and diversity without fragmentation.

Before you leave, ask them – kindly and with a warm smile – not to divide but to collect us and connect each one of us to the whole of society. Encourage them to combine and blend our humble fragments together in the fabric of this world. We may still be random fragments but if you can deliver this message 'To Whom It May Concern', then you can call us *The Blessing Fragments*.

We are one in all and all in one.

Best regards,
a woman who bakes and sells breads
—MOSTAFA RABEA ABDELBASET

Commissioner
Ministry of Culture,
    Arab Republic of Egypt

Curators
Mostafa Rabea Abdelbaset
Mohamad Riad Alhalaby
Amr Allam
Ahmed Essam

Kuressaare central square.
Photo Tiit Veermäe

Põlva central square.
Photo Tõnu Tunnel

Rapla central square.
Photo Siim Solman

Estonia

SQUARE!
POSITIVELY SHRINKING

The exhibition explores the role of high-quality urban space in enhancing the future development perspective of depopulating small towns. It features activities to improve the urban environment with a focus on the redevelopment of central squares within the *Hea avalik ruum* (Great Public Spaces) programme.

The phenomenon of shrinking cities is widespread across Europe and, as a result of the fundamental changes brought about by the 1989–1991 transition period, post-socialist Eastern Europe has been even more affected.

The influence of urbanisation and sub-urbanisation processes in the countries on local communities is often stronger than that of emigration or low birth-rates on the state level. As a result, communities are losing population at a varying pace depending on their size and location. Altogether, 45 Estonian towns out of 47 have lost some of their population since 2000.

The most visible symptoms of shrinkage in urban space are building vacancies and urban brownfields, the predominantly low quality of residential premises, visually unattractive unrenovated buildings, and underinvested environments. An urban space with abandoned and underused buildings has a negative effect on the attitude of residents towards their home. They may lose pride in and loyalty to their town and this, in turn, leads to a lack of initiative to improve it.

Shrinking municipalities need to concentrate on their residents' quality of life. The attractiveness of urban space is important to achieve this goal. Urban space interventions in shrinking communities consist of building demolitions, active housing policy, the restoration of historic buildings, and the revitalisation of urban spaces.

The programme *Hea avalik ruum* is a remarkable example of urban space intervention in shrinking urban areas. The aim of the programme was to renew the centres, main squares as well as the main streets in fifteen Estonian towns by 2020 as a gift from architects to the Republic of Estonia celebrating its 100th anniversary. The town squares in Tõrva, Põlva, Valga and Rapla were completed in 2018, in Võru and Kuressaare in 2019 and Elva and Rakvere in 2020.

Commissioner
Raul Järg,
Estonian Centre
for Architecture

Curators
Jiří Tintěra
Garri Raagmaa
Kalle Vellevoog
Martin Pedanik
Paulina Pähn

Participants
Mari Rass, Ott Alver,
 Alvin Järving,
 Kaidi Põder,
 Helen Rebane,
 Egon Metusala,
 Kaie Kuldkepp,
 Liis Uustal,
 Vilve Enno,
 Gianfranco Franchi,
 Chiara Tesi,
 Rea Sepping
Siiri Vallner,
 Indrek Peil,
 Villem Tomiste;
Häli-Ann Tooms,
 Mari-Liis Männik
Ülle Maiste,
 Diana Taalfeld,
 Anne Saarniit,
 Roomet Helbre,
 Taavi Kuningas
Risto Parve, Kai Süda;
Liisa Hirsch, Patrick
 Tubin McGinley
Anna Hints,
 Joosep Matjus,
 Ants Tammik,
 Tushar Prakash,
 Urmas Reisberg,
 Kairid Laks

Producers
Eve Arpo,
Maria Kristiin Peterson
 (Estonian Centre
 for Architecture)

Collaborators
Mint LIST
Silvia Pärmann

With the Support of
Estonian Ministry
 of Culture
Cultural Endowment
 of Estonia
Rakvere City
 Government
Rapla Municipality
 Government
Võru City
 Government
Valga Municipality
 Government
Elva Municipality
 Government
Põlva Municipality
 Government
Saaremaa Municipality
 Government
Tõrva Municipality
 Government

Puutalo house with its resident in the Pitäjänmäki district of Helsinki, Finland 2020. Photo and © Juuso Westerlund

Puutalo house with its resident in Barranquilla, Colombia 2020. Photo and © Juuso Westerlund

Workers lift a factory-made wall panel into place during the construction of the Marttila neighbourhood in Pitäjänmäki, Helsinki, in 1943. Photo Roos. © Central Archives for Finnish Business Records (ELKA)

A staged photograph shows the furnished interior of a newly completed home in the Jollas neighbourhood of Helsinki, in the mid-1950s. © Central Archives for Finnish Business Records (ELKA)

Finland

NEW STANDARDS

New Standards takes up the question of *How will we live together?* by revisiting the thousands of standard houses that were produced in Finland during and following the Second World War. The project looks at the influence these modest, prefabricated buildings have on architecture, politics, economics, material culture, and domestic life.

The exhibition focuses on the story of Puutalo Oy (Timber Houses Ltd), an industrial enterprise established in 1940 by 21 Finnish timber manufacturing companies.

This unique partnership was born out of crisis when Finland sought to resettle 420,000 Karelian refugees. However, the political and economic impacts of war led these efforts to be quickly redirected toward international export. From 1940 to 1955, Finland sent millions of square meters of buildings to more than 30 countries, helping to define a new standard of living around the world. Focusing on these two decades of production and export, the story illustrates the ways in which architecture connected with industrialisation and international exchange during a period of intense global development.

The exhibition documents this extensive architectural production and its contribution to Finland's international reputation for design and manufacturing. It considers the Puutalo buildings as a model of mass production that raised living standards through quality design while leaving space for individual expression. Drawing from a massive archive of materials, the curators have carefully selected drawings, photographs and advertisements that illustrate the ambitions of this period as well as its architectural legacy. Alongside historical artefacts, a series of newly commissioned photographs show these buildings and their occupants today. The images reveal the ways that these houses are inhabited today, after eight decades of use, repair, and adaptation.

—LAURA BERGER, PHILIP TIDWELL, KRISTO VESIKANSA

Commissioner
Katarina Siltavuori,
Director Archinfo Finland

Curators
Laura Berger
Philip Tidwell
Kristo Vesikansa

Participants
Juuso Westerlund
(commissioned photography)

Exhibition Design
Philip Tidwell

Graphic Design
Päivi Häikiö

Organiser
Archinfo Finland

Head of Communications
Miina Jutila

Project Manager
Sini Parikka

Project Coordinators
Francesco Raccanelli
Lena Kingelin

With the main Support of
Ministry of Education and
Culture, Finland

With the Support of
Ministry of the Environment,
Finland
Dialab
Embassy of Finland in Rome
Helsinki Distilling Company
Kehys- ja kultausliike Ivonen
Mapita
Nikari

Website
Ville Niemi

Learning from SKY, 2012

Cité de Beutre, 2019

Learning from SKY, 2012.
All images © Christophe Hutin

France

The *Communities at work* project proposes an exploration of the intersection between the proficiency of architecture and the performance of inhabitants. This transversal approach to the profession attempts to shed light on the implications of architecture in a rapidly changing contemporary world.

The exhibition takes us on a journey of the mind in architecture, an optimistic view of the world where inhabitant communities are impelled to act on their living environments, their everyday lives. The projects on display are derived not from a formal demonstration, but from an approach of slow and multifaceted transformations. The communities seem to be the most relevant resources for transforming living space, as well as for establishing a spatial contract resulting from bottom-up approaches. The project approach takes into account the performative aspect of the inhabitants, the uses, of life in all its forms, by an architecture that is precise and indeterminate. Improvisation takes place as a possibility of transforming living space considered here as "works in progress".

Through their actions, the communities at work take ownership of their environments and thus establish a space of commonality for the government to discuss their living environment. Faced with human and material wastefulness, we propose a different angle from which to look at the life that is already present everywhere, along with the means of an astute, accurate and tactful strategy to enhance it. We present documentaries on living communities at work on the transformation of their daily environments, in France but also around the world: in Johannesburg, Bordeaux, Detroit, Mérignac, Hanoi... and other instances that we have yet to locate, find like so many gems enlightening us on the capacity of the world to reinvent itself. Analogous situations, by mirror effect, inform us about the phenomena at work, by their deviations from norms and of the standardisation of the world. How do they live together and what spatial contract do they engage in? The lessons learned from these different case studies should give us critical insight into *how we will live together*.

—CHRISTOPHE HUTIN

Commissioner
Ministry of Europe
   and Foreign Affairs
Ministry of Culture
with
Institut Français

Curator
Christophe Hutin

Participants
Inhabitants of GHI du Grand
   Parc in Bordeaux
Cité de transit de Beutre in
   Mérignac (France)
Kliptown in Soweto (South
   Africa)
KTT apartment buildings in
   Hanoi (Vietnam)
Southwest Detroit (USA)

Organiser
Christophe Hutin Architecture

**Audiovisual Associate
Producer**
Grand Angle Productions

Graphic Design
Kubik

Partners
City of Bordeaux
Bordeaux Métropole

Audrey Tang & Lama, 2038

Jennifer Jacquet, Becca Franks & Orca, 2038

Omoju Miller & Audrey Tang, 2038

E. Glen Weyl, 2038

Germany

2038
THE NEW SERENITY

Today, in the year 2038, we have mastered the great crises. It was close, but we made it. The global economic and ecological disasters of the 2020s brought people, states, institutions, and companies together. They committed themselves to fundamental rights and jointly created viable, adaptable systems and legal frameworks on a planetary basis, giving decentralised, local structures the space to maintain and create highly diverse models of co-existing.

Technology and big data helped us to turn new and old ideas into reality. And often it was architects who opened doors and were part of the denouements. Because they had answers instead of coming up with more questions. Drama is now history. We live in a radical democracy, in a radical bureaucracy. On a planet that doesn't know or need heroes or villains.

2038 looks back from the future, trying to understand how we managed to get off one more time, with a black eye. How we achieved a state of 'New Serenity'.

As in *One Thousand and One Nights*, where Sultana Scheherazade keeps designing worlds of co-existence to escape death. An endless scenario–universe of joints, interstices, and storylines. Pretty much what Buckminster Fuller called 'the future'.

Commissioner
Federal Ministry of the Interior, Building and Community

Curator
2038, initiated by
Arno Brandlhuber
Olaf Grawert
Nikolaus Hirsch
Christopher Roth

Participants
Blaise Agüera y Arcas
Leo Altaras
Diana Alvarez-Marin
Andrés Arauz
Arts of the Working Class
Mara Balestrini
Sandra Bartoli
Diann Bauer
Jan Bauer
Tatiana Bilbao
Carl Berthold
Lara Verena Bellenghi
Oana Bogdan
Erik Bordeleau
Mohamed Bourouissa
Jakob Brandtberg
    Knudsen &
    Lorenz von Seidlein
Francesca Bria
Loren Britton
Agnieszka Brzezanska
Vera Bühlmann
Bureau N
Benjamin Burq
Marina Castillo Deball
Vint Cerf
cfk architetti
Kristof Croes
Elke Doppelbauer
Keller Easterling
Tobia de Eccher
Ludwig Engel
Joao Enxuto & Erica Love
ExRotaprint
Manuel Falkenhahn
Jan Fermon
Cosimo Flohr

Foreign Legion
Yona Friedman
Renée Gailhoustet
Jan-Peter Gieseking
Goethe-Institut
Dorothee Hahn
Helene Hegemann
Holger Heissmeyer
Angelika Hinterbrandner
Fabrizio Hochschild
    Drummond
Ludger Hovestadt
Pan Hu
Jennifer Jacquet &
    Becca Franks
Jonas Janke
Mitchell Joachim
Sonja Junkers
Roberta Jurčić
Claudia Kessler
Goda Klumbyte
Gábor Kocsis
Sénamé Koffi Agbodjinou
Ulrich Kriese
Philipp Krüpe
Lukas Kubina
Nikolaus Kuhnert
Phyllis Lambert
Samira Lenzin
Lawrence Lessig
Cédric Libert
Ferdinand Ludwig &
    Daniel Schoenle
Suhail Malik
Charlotte
    Malterre-Barthes
Renzo Martens
Hilary Mason
V. Mitch McEwen
James Meadway
MicroEnergy
    International
Omoju Miller
Konstantin Minnich
Evgeny Morozov
Motif
Motor Productions
Caroline Nevejan
Bahar Noorizadeh
Sabine Oberhuber &

Thomas Rau
Jorge Orozco
Verena Otto
Shwetal Patel
    Wong Ping
Poligonal
Joanna Pope
Christian Posthofen
Leif Randt
Raue
Rebiennale
Kim Stanley Robinson
Denis Jaromil Roio
Raquel Rolnik
Meghan Rolvien
Juliana Rotich
S.a.L.E. Docks
Saygel, Schreiber &
    Gioberti
Clemens Schick
Patrik Schumacher
Jack Self
Max Senges
Deane Simpson,
    Space-time.tv
Sorry Press
Jonas Staal
Bruce Sterling
Michael Stöppler
Lia Strenge
Audrey Tang
TerraO
The Laboratory of
    Manuel Bürger
Cassie Thornton
Jeanne Tremsal
Galaad Van Daele
Iris van der Tuin
Marcus Vesterager
Julian Wäckerlin
Eyal Weizman
Julia Werlen
E. Glen Weyl
Why Ventures
Mark Wigley
Anna Yeboah
Vanessa Yeboah
Erez Yoeli
Tirdad Zolghadr
and many more...

The Garden of Privatised Delights, 2020. Concept collage.
Image Unscene Architecture

The Garden of Privatised Delights, 2020. Concept collage.
Image Unscene Architecture

Play With(out) Grounds, 2020. Concept collage.
Image vPPR

Great Britain

THE GARDEN OF PRIVATISED DELIGHTS

The *Garden of Privatised Delights* calls for new models of privately owned public space in cities across the UK. It challenges the polarisation of private and public, which often leads to divisions within society. Instead it asks how architects can work with the public to invent new frameworks to improve use, access, and ownership of Britain's public spaces.

In the spirit of Hieronymus Bosch's triptych painting *The Garden of Earthly Delights*, the British Pavilion explores the diversity of privatised public space. Just as Bosch explored the middle ground of Earth between the extremes of Heaven and Hell, privatised public space also sits between two extremes: the utopia of common land before the Enclosures Act of the eighteenth century and the dystopia of total privatisation. Addressing the theme *How will we live together* the pavilion discusses the role of the architect in bringing the public and private sectors together along with other stakeholders to rethink what privatised public space could be.

Privatised public space is widely associated with gated squares in new developments, yet it is a typology that is rooted in British culture, from interior spaces like the pub, to networks dependent on multiple public and private uses like the high street. The global pandemic and recent lockdowns have both highlighted the importance of accessible public space and also the inequalities within society. To explore how to redress this imbalance, the British Pavilion is transformed into a series of immersive spaces under threat like the youth centre, and inaccessible enclaves like the garden square, each overlaid with proposals for how they can be re-programmed, revitalised, and opened up. The British Pavilion will generate a new body of research which will engage in the international debate about inclusive and accessible cities, while imagining a future where all public spaces are designed as gardens of delight.

—MADELEINE KESSLER AND MANIJEH VERGHESE, UNSCENE ARCHITECTURE

Commissioner
Sevra Davis,
  Director of
  Architecture,
  Design and Fashion
  at the British
  Council

Curators
Manijeh Verghese
  and Madeleine
  Kessler, Unscene
  Architecture

Participants
Unscene Architecture
The Decorators
Built Works
Studio Polpo
Public Works
vPPR

Organisation
British Council

**Engineering
Consultancy**
Buro Happold

**Lighting and
Interaction Design**
ARUP

**Production
Management**
Install Archive

Graphic Design
Kellenberger-White

**Pavilion Management
and Installation**
M+B Studio

Structural Engineer
Zero4Uno

Planting
Benetazzo
  Spazioverde

Fabrication
The White Wall
  Company
Adventure Playground
  Engineers

With the Support of
ARUP
Sto
Therme Art
Zumtobel

**With the additional
Support of**
Buro Happold
Finsa UK Ltd
2B Heard

**Fellowship
Programme Support**
Foster + Partners
HTA Design LLP

**With kind assistance
from**
Clayworks
Forbo Flooring Systems
K-array
LED Linear™ GmbH
Light Forms
  Architectural
  Lighting
NERI, S.S.
Precision Lighting Ltd
Richter lighting
  technologies GmbH.
WISA Plywood
The White Wall
  Company

Model of Aristotle axis based on the original plan.
Source: School of Architecture, Aristotle University of Thessaloniki

Aerial view of Aristotle Square, 1984.
© Giorgos Tsaousakis

The portico at Aristotle Square, 2018.
© Nikos Kalogirou

Greece

'BOULEVARD DE LA SOCIÉTÉ DES NATIONS', A.K.A. THE ARISTOTLE AXIS IN THESSALONIKI

Designing spaces that encourage 'living together' requires the understanding of historical, geographical, and cultural particularities. The Aristotle axis in Thessaloniki is an expression of European urban design adapted to the regional aspects of the cultural coexistence of locals, migrants, and refugees. In the plan (1918–1921) of the French architect Ernest Hébrard, the axis was called the Boulevard de la Société des Nations according to the political vision of Eleuthèrios Venizèlos and Alexandros Papanastasiou. A relevant research project and workshop were undertaken by academic staff and students of the School of Architecture, Aristotle University of Thessaloniki.

Two parallel exhibitions, in Venice and in Thessaloniki, are connected through a digital interface. Thus, cyberspace emerges as a place of coexistence and conjunction of people of late modernity. The Greek participation accepts the invitation to 'live together' literally and metaphorically, featuring an analytical part in situ and a socio-visual part in the Greek pavilion.

The public axis was actually realised in a different manner from the one envisioned by its creators. Today, it emerges as an emblematic urban condenser, encompassing the entire social pyramid from sought-after apartments on the coastal front to the areas above Egnatia, where many refugees and immigrants are housed. Contemporary commercial and leisure areas, traditional markets (bazaars), hotels, entertainment venues, banks, and public organisations are all developed along its length. Its particular unified, contemporary architectural style is completed by the palimpsest of the unique Roman, Byzantine, and Ottoman monuments revealed along it. Furthermore, Aristotle boulevard distinctively incorporates unique public spaces, squares, paths, and green areas, which both encourage and host political events, cultural activities, exchanges, and informal contact between and among citizens – both permanent residents and nomads. It is an ideal habitat for interactions, a living room of the city, where multiple political, social, and cultural groups are accommodated and coexist.
—NIKOS KALOGIROU

Commissioners
Dimitris Oikonomou,
Deputy Minister of
  Environment and Energy, in
  charge of Regional Planning
  and Urban Environment,
  Ministry of the Environment
  & Energy/Greece (October
  2019–January 2021)
Efthimios Bakogiannis,
  Secretary General for
  Regional Planning and
  Urban Environment,
  Ministry of the Environment
  & Energy/Greece (since
  February 2021)

Curators and Participants
Nikos Kalogirou
Themistoklis
  Chatzigiannopoulos
Maria Dousi
Dimitrios Kontaxakis
Sofoklis Kotsopoulos
Dimitrios Thomopoulos

Grenada House of Parliament, Volumes, 2019.
Photo Kari Outram

Grenada House of Parliament, Entry Forecourt, 2019.
Photo Michael Straley

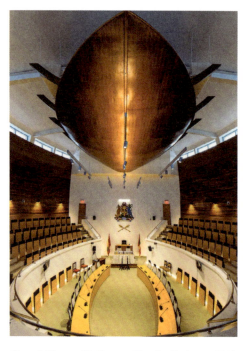

Grenada House of Parliament, Chamber Sculpture, 2019.
Photo Khari Outram

Grenada

COETHOS

COethos is a voice from within Grenada that heralds a new cultural, economic, and social perspective as a way to live locally in relation to rising environmental global issues. *COethos* is a vision, a narrative, where the individual parts are staunchly interdependent and the already completed House of Parliament is the capstone. The future project endows the old town of St George's with a new narrative and enhances it as a central place where the community recognises and proclaims its own unique identity. The reconfiguration of St George's urban landscape, its buildings and forts, and the rejuvenation of key components of Market Square and Carenage, the management of its infrastructures and its motorised and pedestrian traffic, if realised, will eventually benefit every individual.

Grenada is almost the southernmost island of the Caribbean paradise, the last of a series of gems in a crown that softly fades before meeting the continent of South America. A marvel floating above the surface of the water, it is a mirage. Alongside the beauty looms an ever-present threat: waves rise with global warming, winds threaten to destroy its surface and forest, tectonic plates move and quake in a slow dance, and magma boils muffled in the underwater silence.

Inhabiting this land produces the most extraordinarily resilient relics – its people. Grenada, like Venice, is a paradise suspended between a solid historical identity and an uncertain and fragile future. Similarly, its environmental conditions are the cause of both its quality and the weaknesses that undermine the solidity of its paradisiac image. The resilience of its people to rebuild time and time again after each catastrophe is the impetus of the architect to provide a living, breathing, dynamic, urban design that will serve the people well.

COethos interrupts time and simultaneously stretches it: Grenada and its House of Parliament become the place where the geological ages and a community's identity meet. It is the expression of the dynamic ways of inhabiting an unpredictable land, it suspends time and the fragility of the environment while acknowledging them as part of its existence.

Commissioner
Susan Mains

Curators
Marco Ballarin
Stefano Tornieri
Massimo Triches
(Babau Bureau)

Participant
Caribbean Office
   of Co-operative
   Architecture,
   Bryan W. Bullen

Collaborators
Sharon Bidaisee
Irina Kostka
Michael Julien

Pavilion Management
Luisa Flora,
Officina delle Zattere

Technical Support
Fulvio Caputo,
C and C architettura ingegneria

Research
Asher Mains

With the Support of
The Ministry of Culture,
   Grenada
Cymat
Act--Art
Design Grenada

Othernity – Reconditioning Our Modern Heritage,
Installations of the *Showroom,* 2021.
Photo © Dániel Dömölky

Hungary

OTHERNITY – RECONDITIONING OUR MODERN HERITAGE

What lessons could be learnt from architectural Modernism, the legacy of an often-disputed era, confronted today by changing expectations of sustainability, social norms, and (as far as Central and Eastern Europe specifically are concerned) political transformation? What will be the future of these buildings, which comprise a great part of our architectural heritage? *Othernity*, the exhibition of the Hungarian pavilion, offers thought-provoking proposals in response to these questions, by emerging practices from the region.

Europe's former Eastern Bloc possesses a unique local modernist architectural heritage. These buildings were created for a bygone era and society, with limited resources but with great determination and ideals. Instead of simply demolishing this heritage, it should serve as the groundwork for developing a responsible and innovative mode of operation for future architectural practice. Even if this requires changing how we think about heritage, values, and protection.

We invited twelve emerging practices from Central and Eastern Europe to recondition twelve socialist modernist buildings in Budapest. The exhibiting architects' generation is the first that has neither any direct experience of socialism nor any memory of the architectural production methods of that era. At the same time, they were raised among these buildings and they have common experiences and memories of these socialist environments, whether they are from Warsaw, Bratislava, Belgrade, Tallinn, Skopje, Zagreb, Cracow, Bucharest, or Prague.

The Hungarian pavilion of the 17th International Architecture Exhibition highlights both the individual values of the original buildings and the unusual, innovative results of this collaborative research and design process as an attempt to offer new perspectives on the disputed heritage of an era.

We see this project as a new, collaborative method to rethink our ways of heritage protection, as an example for a more experimental architectural community and a more perceptive society.

How will we live together?, asks Hashim Sarkis, chief Curator. Our answer is that we will live together by using what we have, but in a more understanding, innovative, and emotional way. Twelve ways, in fact.

Commissioner
Julia Fabényi

Curator
Dániel Kovács

Participants
A-A Collective
    (Poland, Denmark,
    Switzerland)
Architecture
    Uncomfortable
    Workshop
    (Hungary)
b210 (Estonia)
BUDCUD (Poland)
KONNTRA (Slovenia,
    North-Macedonia,
    Croatia)
MADA (Serbia)
MNPL Workshop
    (Ukraine)
Paradigma Ariadné
    (Hungary)
PLURAL (Slovakia);
Vojtěch Rada
    (Czechia)
LLRRLLRR (Estonia,
    United Kingdom)
Studio Act (Romania)

Curatorial Team
Attila Róbert Csóka
Szabolcs Molnár
Dávid Smiló

Organisation
Ludwig Museum -
    Museum of
    Contemporary Art,
    Budapest

Project Coordination
Géza Boros
Anna Bálványos
Zsigmond Lakó

Communication
Zsuzsanna Fehér
Gabriella Rothman

Graphic Design
Marcell Kazsik

Curatorial Assistant
Laura Sütöri

Chief Technician
Béla Bodor

With the Support of
Hungarian Ministry
    of Human
    Capacities

Website
othernity.eu

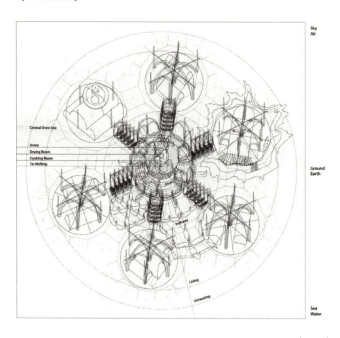

The Ark Re-Imagined - Schematic Drawing

Rashad Salim with George Stewart, *The Ark Envisioned*, 2020. Photography and architectural drawing.
Courtesy George Stewart (architectural drawing). © Rashad Salim

Rashad Salim, *The Ark Re-imagined / Atlas Ark*, 2019. Digital photomontage.
Courtesy Khalid Ramzi and Rand Al-Shakarchi (architectural drawing); Nicolò Di Giovanni
(photography); Kuba Rudzinski / Edge of Arabia (photo-editing). © Rashad Salim

Iraq

ARK RE-IMAGINED: THE EXPEDITIONARY PAVILION

As Iraq's first participation in the Biennale Architettura, the *Ark Re-imagined* returns to the very beginning of Iraq's architectural legacy: the vernacular architecture and watercraft of ancient Mesopotamia, exemplifying a seminal 'alphabet of making' that set the stage for civilisation to emerge.

Our project is fundamentally art led, employing the forms and processes of art, attending to aesthetics and beauty in the context of the architecture of movement. Our primeval ancestors were explorers; systems of shelter and transportation that facilitated movement were essential tools.

We re-imagine the Ark as an organic, tensile-built, fractal structure, composed of modular units derived from vernacular architecture, craft techniques, and boat types attributable to the late Neolithic/early Chalcolithic periods as experienced in the Gulf region from the Mesopotamian watershed to the straits of Hormuz. The techniques are universal; what defines such an Ark as specifically Mesopotamian is the regional ecology and material cultural heritage.

The mission of this Ark is to gather resources and people, convening dialogue through an architecture of cooperative engagement. The challenge implicit in the question *How will we live together?* is particularly pertinent for Iraq in the present moment of turbulent change and with a globally dispersed diaspora.

Our *expeditionary pavilion* engages dynamically with its locality and our Venetian partners, exploring links between Venice's wetland environment and that of southern Iraq. We investigate boats, from prehistoric origins to the apex of design as manifest in both the Venetian boating tradition and the disappearing boats of Basra's canals and marshes.

Like Venice, southern Iraq is now facing the critical challenge of the Anthropocene, a climate event comparable to the ancient Flood (sea level rise between the Pleistocene and Holocene). The Flood's impact upon ancient Mesopotamia arguably set in motion the cultural process that has led us here.

Drawing on experiential archaeology, we enquire beyond the relics of civilisation, into the transformative processes that shaped human culture and remain relevant to our emerging future.

—RASHAD SALIM AND SAFINA PROJECTS

Commissioner
Ministry of Culture

Curators
Safina Projects
Edge of Arabia

Participant
Rashad Salim

Organisation
Reale Società Canottieri Bucintoro, exhibition hosts and workshop collaborators
University of Baghdad, Association for Conserving Architectural Heritage, architectural design and modelling
TFIU Healing Arts Initiative, co-programming
Factum Foundation, digital technology consultants
University of Al-Qadisiyah, Basra Museum, URIM Initiative, Università della Sapienza di Roma, content contributors

With the Support of
ALIPH Foundation
Arab Fund for Arts and Culture
Arab Council for the Social Sciences
British Council's Cultural Protection Fund, in partnership with DCMS
Makiya-Kufa Charity
Nahrein Network (AHRC and UCL)

Annex, *Entanglement 01*, 2020. Thermographic Still

Ireland

ENTANGLEMENT

Commissioner
Culture Ireland

Curators and Participants
Annex
(Sven Anderson,
Alan Butler, David Capener,
Donal Lally, Clare Lyster,
Fiona McDermott)

With the Support of
Ireland at Venice is an
initiative of Culture Ireland
in partnership with the Arts
Council and in 2021 the
pavilion also has the support of:
The Department of Tourism,
    Culture, Arts, Gaeltacht,
    Sport and Media
Department of Housing, Local
    Government and Heritage
Royal Institute of Architects
    Ireland
TU Dublin School of Creative
    Arts
TU Dublin Graduate School of
    Creative Arts and Media
Trinity College Dublin
CONNECT Research Centre
    for Future Networks and
    Communications
University of Illinois at
    Chicago, Creative Activity
    Award
ARUP
Valentia Slate, Office of Public
    Works and Green on Red
    Gallery

The digital is material. In 2016, IBM announced that 90% of the world's data had been produced in the prior two years. This recent and rapid exponential growth of global data now reveals itself locally across the Irish landscapes as a vast constellation of data centres, fibre optic cable networks, and energy infrastructures. In 2019, Dublin overtook London as the data centre hub of Europe. By the year 2027, data centres are forecast to consume 31% of Ireland's total electricity demand. The ecological footprint of the cloud has now become a significant focus. For Ireland, this aspect of the data infrastructure story is nothing new. The first transatlantic telegraph cable, at 3,200 km in length and landing at Valentia Island on the West Coast of Ireland in the mid-nineteenth century, was insulated by a Malaysian latex, driving the Palaquium Gutta-Percha tree to near extinction. The Irish pavilion, titled *Entanglement*, avoids the crutch of utopian fantasy by looking at data infrastructure in the present, and in its most real, material sense. Foregrounding the materiality of our digital age, *Entanglement* subverts a fundamental typology of the network, the server cabinet, to uncloud the sleek aesthetic of an industry, which is forming our realities. The Irish pavilion presents a structure that performs a collapse of the local and planetary scale data infrastructure networks into the most primitive of socialising technologies – the bonfire – to draw attention to and reframe how we comprehend the data infrastructure already around us.

Untitled (Cow Lifted to Ship), Unknown year and photographer.
The Arvin Yacobi Negative Prints Collection.
Courtesy and © The Central Zionist Archives

Water Buffaloes in the Hulah Valley, 1935. Unknown photographer.
Courtesy and © the KKL-JNF Photo Archive

A Lesson on the Honey Bee at Mikve Israel, 1937.
Photo Zoltan Kluger.
Courtesy and © Israel State Archives

Israel

LAND. MILK. HONEY.

The exhibition *Land of Milk and Honey - the Construction of Plenitude* examines the reciprocal relations between humans, animals, and the environment within the Israeli context.

The protagonists of the exhibition are animals, both wild and domesticated. The setting is the land of milk of honey, the region stretching between the Jordan River and the Mediterranean Sea, a place many imagine as holy and promised; the much-contested territory of both Israel and Palestine.

The phrase 'land of milk and honey' has been used to describe this area for millennia. It first appeared in the Old Testament and has become a common metaphor for plenitude and prosperity. However, there was often an enormous gap between the way people pictured the land from afar, and how they experienced it upon arrival.

Shortly after the British colonisation of Palestine in 1917, and more vigorously after the founding of the state of Israel in 1948, efforts were initiated in order to transform the local landscape to better fit European ideals of abundance. Within a few decades the territory experienced far-reaching environmental changes due to initiatives in agronomy, engineering, architecture, and legislation. Thus, the land of milk and honey turned from a religious promise to an action plan: fresh water springs were pumped and channelled for irrigation, wetlands drained and reconstructed as agricultural fields, whole areas went through intensive afforestation processes, and animal bodies were manipulated into food-producing machines. Urbanisation, infrastructure, and mechanised agriculture reshaped the environment.

The successful metamorphosis of the region into prosperous agricultural lands came at the cost of irreparable damage to the local fauna and flora, as well as the disruption of habitats.

Through five case studies – cows, goats, honey bees, water buffaloes, and bats – we construct a spatial history of a place in five acts: Mechanisation; Territory; Cohabitation; Extinction; and Post-Human. We thus offer a zoocentric analysis of a land radically transformed by the powers of ideology, religion, and technology.

Commissioners
Michael Gov
Arad Turgeman

Curators
Dan Hasson
Iddo Ginat
Rachel Gottesman
Yonatan Cohen
Tamar Novick

Participants
Dan Hasson
Iddo Ginat
Rachel Gottesman
Yonatan Cohen
Tamar Novick
Netta Laufer
Shadi Habib Allah
Daniel Meir
Apollo Legisamo
Adam Havkin

Curatorial Advisor
Yael Messer

Scientific Research
Tamar Novick

Project Team
Shira Yasur
Bar Mussan Levi
Omri Levy
Tamar Ofer
Idan Sidi
Michael Cidor
Eran Amir
Maya Dann

Photography
Gili Merin
Sarale Gur Lavi
Aviad Bar Ness

Progetto grafico
Studio Gimel2

Scientific Advisors
The Steinhardt
    Museum of Natural
    History, Israel
    National Center
    for Biodiversity
    Studies, Tel Aviv
    University

Collaborators
The Steinhardt
    Museum of Natural
    History, Israel
    National Center
    for Biodiversity
    Studies, Tel Aviv
    University
Centre de recherche
    français à Jérusalem
    (CRFJ) UMIFRE
    7 - USR 3132

With the Support of
Israel Ministry of
    Culture and
    Sport, Museums
    and Visual Arts
    Department
Israel Ministry of
    Foreign Affairs,
    Cultural Diplomacy
    Bureau
Mifal HaPais Council
    for the Culture and
    Arts
Anatta
Ronny Douek
Liebling Haus, The
    White City Center
    Tel Aviv-Yafo

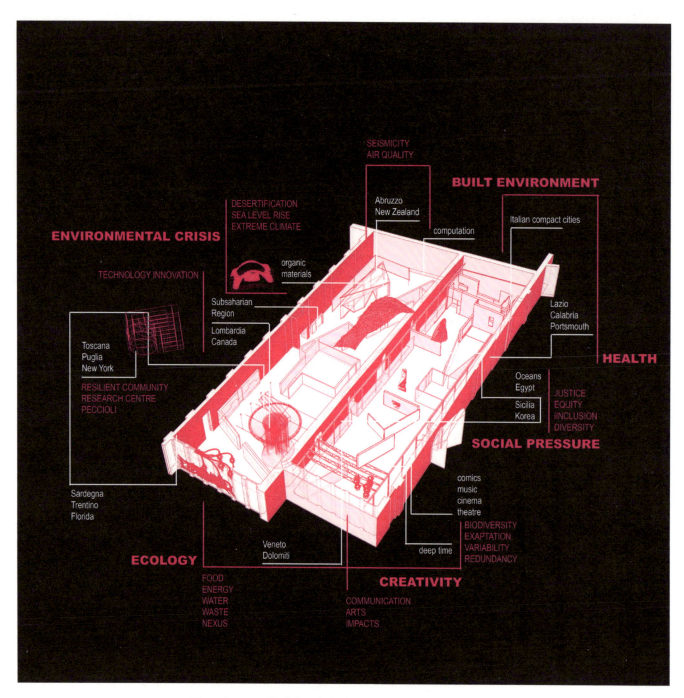

The carbon neutral Padiglione Italia. Axonometric projection illustrating the reuse of 80% of plaster-wall structures from the 2019 Padiglione Italia and the recovery/recycling of the remaining 20%

Italy

COMUNITÀ RESILIENTI – RESILIENT COMMUNITIES

Commissioner
Onofrio Cutaia,
Director-General
for Contemporary
Creativity, Ministry
of Culture

Curator
Alessandro Melis

Ministry of Culture

Minister of Culture
Dario Franceschini

**Under Secretary of
State**
Lucia Borgonzoni

Head of the Cabinet
Lorenzo Casini

General Secretary
Salvatore Nastasi

**Head of Press
Office and
Communications**
Mattia Morandi

**Directorate-General
for Contemporary
Creativity**

Director General
Onofrio Cutaia

Director Unit 1
Cultural and creative
enterprises, fashion
and design
Fabio De Chirico

Director Unit 2
Contemporary Art
Sandra Suatoni

Director Unit 3
Contemporary
Architecture
Luca Maggi

General coordination
Luciano Antonino
Scuderi

**Director-General
Staff**
Maria Luisa Amante
Eva Barrera

Secretary
Roberta Gaglione
Support staff
Sara Airò
Chiara Francesconi
Antonella Lucarelli
Claudia Vitiello

Administration
Graziella D'Urso
Giovanna Terranova
Support staff
Adriano Decina
Riccardo Di Pretoro
Palmiro Antonio
Esposito

**Communication and
Press Office**
Silvia Barbarotta
Francesca Galasso

Thanks to
Esmeralda Valente
for the General
coordination
in the years
2019-2020

Padiglione Italia

Production
La Biennale di
Venezia

Commissioner
Onofrio Cutaia

Curator
Alessandro Melis

Deputy Curator
Benedetta Medas

Exhibition Sections

*Concept Architectural
Exaptation*
Alessandro Melis
Telmo Pievani

*Architectural
exaptation*
Alessandro Melis
Benedetta Medas
Paola Corrias
Alice Maccanti

Dolomiti Care
Gianluca D'Inca Levis

*Decolonising the built
environment*
RebelArchitette
Alessandro Melis

*DESING(ING): dal
cucchiaio alla città*
Paolo Di Nardo
Francesca Tosi

*Architecture as
caregiver*
Antonino Di Raimo
Maria Perbellini
Cressida Bowyer

Sud Globale
Paola Ruotolo

*Università, agenzie di
resilienza*
Maurizio Carta
Paolo Di Nardo

Storia di un minuto
Alessandro Gaiani
Emilia Giorgi

Guido Incerti
Italian Best Practice
Gian Luigi Melis
Margherita Baldocchi
Benedetta Medas

Laboratorio Peccioli
Ilaria Fruzzetti
Nico Panizzi
Laura Luperi

Ecologia Tacita
Ingrid Paoletti

*Resilienza, paesaggio
e arte*
Annacaterina Piras
Emanuele Montibeller
Giacomo Bianchi
Laura Tomaselli

Giardino delle Vergini
Dario Pedrabissi

*Arti Industriali e
Creative – Sezione
crossover*
Benedetta Medas,
Monica Battistoni,
Dana Hamdan,
Antonio Lara-
Hernandez

DataFrame
Guido Robazza,
Filippo Lovato,
Gustavo Romanillos
Assistenti:
Aina Barcelo,
Dana Hamdan
Immagini Copernicus:
IUSS Pavia – CIRTA
Research Centre,
Andrea Taramelli,
Emiliana Valentini,
Margherita Righini,
Laura Piedelobo,
Emma Schiavon,
Clara Armaroli

**Mapping Resilient
Communities**
Luisa Bravo
with Roberta
Franceschinelli,
Fondazione Unipolis,
Simone D'Antonio,
ANCI – National
point URBACT Italy

in collaboration
with City Space
Architecture e UN-
Habitat, the program
on human settlements
of the United Nations

Installation Design
Heliopolis 21

**Project
Management**
Gian Luigi Melis,
Alessandro Melis
with Paolo Di Nardo,
Simone Chietti, Liam
Donovan-Stumbles,
Barbora Foerster,
Ilaria Fruzzetti,
Dana Hamdan,
Laura Luperi, Filippo
Mariani, Nico Panizzi

**Management
sponsor and relations
with companies**
Simone Chietti

**Project
Collaboration**
Margherita Baldocchi
Monica Battistoni
Pietro De Pasca,
Alice Maccanti
Benedetta Medas
Lorenzo Parrini
Roberto Poziello
Martina Mancini
Lorenzo Pucci

**Communication
Coordination**
Paolo Arrigoni

Social Media
Benedetta Medas,
Antonio Lara-
Hernandez,
Nicoletta Podda

**Website, Design and
Video Production**
Dirty Work,
Web design-Grafica-
Comunicazione

Graphic Design
DoKC Lab / Ercolani
Bros.

Catalogue
D Editore

Catalogue Curators
Alessandro Melis,
Benedetta Medas
Telmo Pievani

**Editing and
Translation
Coordination**
Tommaso Castellana
Paola Corrias
Claire Coulter
Barbora Melis
Benedetta Medas
Athena Pagnozzi
Emmanuele J. Pilia
Alice Piras
Gabriele Presta
Greta Salvetti
Viviana Urciuoli
Sergio Vivaldi

**Steering Committee
Comunità Resilienti**
Katia Accossato
Marilena Baggio
Paola Boarin
Luisa Bravo
Carla Brisotto
Maurizio Carta
Luca D'Acci
Ingrid Paoletti
Daniela Perrotti
Luigi Trentin

Scientific Advisory
Roberto Aloisio
Barry Bergdoll
Lisa Bodei
Carla Broccardo
Roberto Buizza
Daniela Ciccarelli
Eugenio Coccia
Elena Cologni
Inanna Hamati-Ataya
Claudia Maraston
Piergiorgio Odifreddi
Michela Passalacqua
Michele Punturo
Saskia Sassen
Richard Sennet
Guido Tonelli
David Turnbull

Advisory Board
Fabrizio Aimar, Besnik
Aliaj, Thomas Auer,

Mauro Baracco,
Edgardo Bolio Arceo,
Marco Brizzi, Julia
Brown, Angela Bruni,
Leonardo Caffo,
Jeffrey Andrew
Carney, William
Carpenter, Fitnat
Cimsit Kos, Pamela
Cole, Claire Coulter,
Virginia Cucchi,
Simone D'Antonio,
Chiara de' Rossi,
Lidia Decandia,
Cristina Donati,
Elena Douvlou,
Jorge Esquivel,
Alessandra Ferrari,
Simona Finessi,
Julia Gatley, Tomas
Ghisellini, Elena
Granata, Martin Haas,
Ornella Iuorio, Yazid
Mohammed Khemri,
Alessandra Lai, Steffen
Lehmann, Fabiano
Lemes De Oliveira,
Elena Manferdini,
Alessandro Marata,
Ludovico Marinò,
Walter Mayrhofer,
Milena Metalkova,
Belinda Mitchell,
Consuelo Nava,
Francesco Palazzo,
Giulia Pellegri, Maria
Perbellini, Paola
Pierotti, Elisa Poli,
Luigi Prestinenza
Puglisi, Anna Quinz,
Sonja Radovic,
Valentina Radi,
Stefano Renzoni,
Diego Repetto,
Mosè Ricci, Lorenzo
Ricciarelli, Agatino
Rizzo, Catsou
Roberts, Heather
Rumble, Nicoletta
Sale, Luca Sgrilli,
Stefano Sodi,
Alessandro Spennato,
Thomas Spiegelhalter,
Giulia Tambato, Sara
Vegni, Elisa Visconti,
Angioletta Voghera

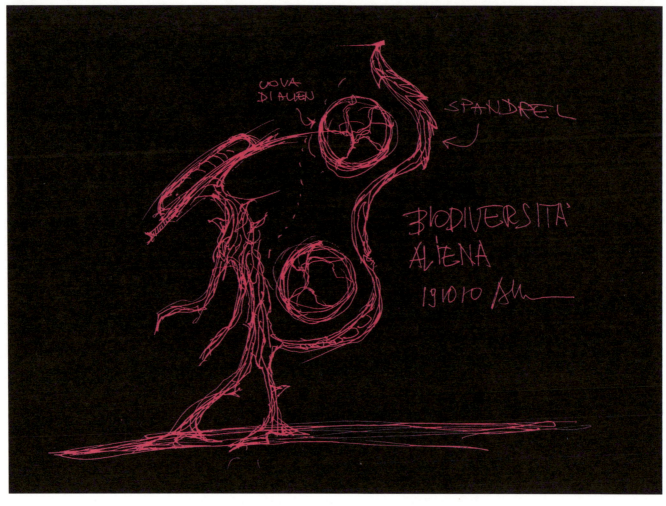

Resilience and transdisciplinarity. Initial sketch for curatorial installation
Spandrel, inspired by research of palaeontologist Stephen J. Gould, 1979

Resilience and transdisciplinarity. Initial sketch for the curatorial
installation *Genoma*, inspired by research of Ewan Birney
(EMBL's European Bioinformatics Institute)

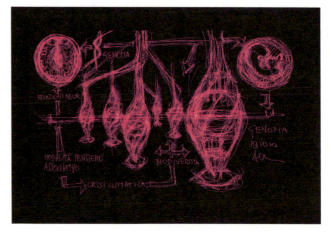

Resilience and transdisciplinarity. Sketch for the *Genoma* installation
as element linking the biological sciences and creative arts

Architecture must make a significant contribution to improving the quality of life of all citizens, particularly at a time when we are being forced to face challenges of unprecedented proportions and urgency like those arising from climate change and the global pandemic. This is why the Ministry of Culture, through its Directorate-General for Contemporary Creativity, has promoted a research laboratory at the 2021 Italy Pavilion, for a multidisciplinary and shared reflection on these issues.

Curated by Hashim Sarkis, the 17th International Architecture Exhibition - La Biennale di Venezia investigates how, in the context of widening political divides and growing economic inequalities, we might imagine spaces in which we can generously live together.

In keeping with the proposed themes, Minister of Culture Dario Franceschini took account of the general theme of the show and supported the work of Alessandro Melis, curator of 2021 Italian Pavilion. Titled *Resilient Communities*, the Pavilion sets out a reflection on Italian communities and their ability to transform and adapt, as has become necessary to respond locally to global challenges. Within twenty years, our peripheries will have to transform increasingly into resilient communities, capable of positively combating modern-day social and environmental pressure. The Italian city is a model of excellence to be drawn upon for rethinking urban peripheries, which are now priority areas of complexity and risk for the country. And for them, strategies of use for dealing with the unprecedented problems architecture will have to grapple with must be found, in a necessarily transversal, multidisciplinary perspective.

These are the challenges that the 2021 Italian pavilion launches for the entire community: capitalizing on a heritage of knowledge, starting from the principles and the form of the compact and ecological Italian city; spreading the results of applied research even outside of disciplinary and academic settings; and a commitment to the concrete involvement of all levels of governance, from national, regional, and local institutions to civil society and active citizenship.
—ONOFRIO CUTAIA
COMMISSIONER, PADIGLIONE ITALIA 2021
DIRECTOR-GENERAL FOR CONTEMPORARY CREATIVITY, MINISTRY OF CULTURE

Comunità resilienti – Resilient Communities

The *Comunità resilienti – Resilient Communities* project places the question of climate change, in all its dramatic force, at the centre of the exhibition. In particular, it aims to underline how in Italy climate change is sorely testing the agricultural system and the production of high-quality food which are at heart of Italy's urban model. The curatorial project, in its choral specificity of harmoniously qualified spirits and voices, is founded on the firm conviction that architecture, now devoid of dated prerogatives that saw it as an autonomous discipline, must significantly contribute to the improvement of the quality of life we lead, offering adequate and credible answers to the new environmental and social changes.

The pavilion's main objective, therefore, is to reflect on the resilience of communities, intended as an imperative interpretative key for the recuperation of a new form of centrality between the productive territory and urban space, a field within which we can re-find an adequate answer to the many challenges that impinge on all our lives and the life of generations to come.

The space we have devised is itself a resilient community, in turn constituted by 'subcommunities' represented by individual sections, intended therefore as a laboratory, a research centre, or a case study, according to two paradigms: a reflexion on the state of art on the theme of urban resilience in Italy and the world through an exhibition of works by eminent Italian architects; and a focus on new methodologies, innovation, research, and interdisciplinary experiments between architecture and botany, agronomy, biology, and medicine. From the very outset, our desire was to give life to a pavilion that offers a choral response to the pressing environmental and social challenges of the world we live in, a response that will continue to live in time and space even after the prestigious Venetian exhibition has come to a close. The extensive calendar of international appointments and the number of prestigious partners from the five continents who will participate in the panels of the *Comunità resilienti – Resilient Communities* space are only the first element of a commitment that, personally, assumes the passionate form of urgency, truth, and justice within an aesthetic vision that – this is our hope – will attract and stimulate the imagination of a broad and youthful public who are attentive to the common cause.
—ALESSANDRO MELIS
CURATOR PADIGLIONE ITALIA 2021

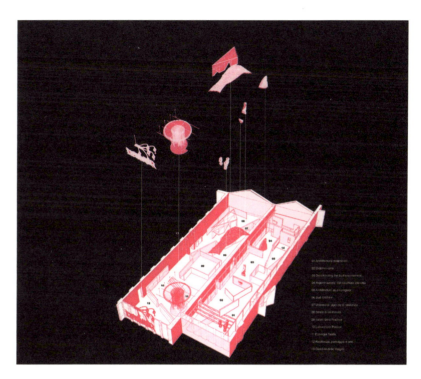

Resilience and transdisciplinarity. The Italian pavilion as a laboratory.
Axonometric projection illustrating insertion of functional
installations or prototypes

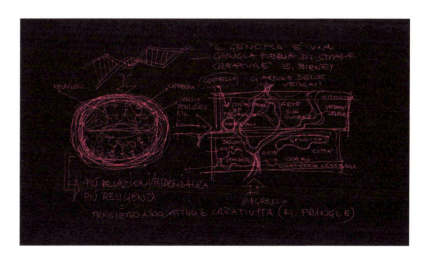

Resilience and creativity. Initial sketch for project as 'Jungle filled
with strange creatures' (www.zeit.de/2012/37/Encode-Projekt-Birney)

All images © DDAA + village°

Japan

CO-OWNERSHIP OF ACTION: TRAJECTORIES OF ELEMENTS

Your actions are not yours alone. Every action, however trivial, is the outcome of countless cumulative actions born of our relations with one another. So it is absurd to claim that our actions belong solely to ourselves.

We are exhibiting a wooden house of a type that is extremely commonplace in Japan. One consequence of the country's declining population – a harbinger for the rest of the world? – is a shockingly large number of houses that, having exceeded their life expectancy, simply await demolition. We are moving one such house to Venice to exhibit at this year's 17th International Architecture Exhibition.

Once in Venice, the house will not retain its original form. Having been dismantled to fit into containers for shipping, its various elements will find new uses at the exhibition – as display walls, as benches, as projection screens, and so on. Reassembling the fragmented house on-site into diverse configurations will give new life to these elements.

However, many elements will inevitably be lost in the course of dismantling, shipping, and reassembling the house. The architects and artisans from Japan who travel to Venice to revive and rebuild the house will compensate for its missing elements with new or locally obtained materials. The process will be shared via the internet so as to pass the work on to successive teams of architects and artisans. Though this collaboration may resemble cloud-based documentary film editing, it will be missing the concept of 'completion': the work is to continue for the duration of the exhibition.

What we will be displaying here is the actual process by which multiple architects and artisans collaborate to produce a chimera-like installation that combines old and new materials in composite forms. The trajectories traced by the elements of this house will testify to the way our actions are part of a continuum: rooted in the past, linked to the future, and owned by all of us.

Commissioner
The Japan Foundation

Curator
Kozo Kadowaki

Participants
Jo Nagasaka
Ryoko Iwase
Toshikatsu Kiuchi
Taichi Sunayama
Daisuke Motogi
Rikako Nagashima

Researchers
Norimasa Aoyagi
Aya Hiwatashi
Naoyuki Matsumoto
Tetsu Makino
Building System Design
    Laboratory at Meiji
    University (Kozo Kadowaki,
    Makoto Isono, Kimihito Ito)

Editor
Jiro Iio

Advisor
Kayoko Ota

Photo
Jan Vranovský

Film
Hirofumi Nakamoto

Exhibition Design
Schemata Architects
    (Jo Nagasaka, Yuhei Yagi)
Studio IWASE |
    Architecture+Landscape
    (Ryoko Iwase, Kaoru Endo)
sunayama studio + Toshikatsu
    Kiuchi Architect (Taichi
    Sunayama, Toshikatsu
    Kiuchi, Risako Okuizumi,
    Kei Machida/Zu Architects)
DDAA (Daisuke Motogi,
    Riku Murai)

Graphic Design
village* (Rikako Nagashima,
    Kohei Kawaminami,
    Hiroyuki Inada)

Structural Engineering
TECTONICA (Yoshinori
    Suzuki, Kakeru Tsuruta)
Mitsuhiro Kanada Studio at
    Tokyo University of the Arts
    (Mitsuhiro Kanada)

Exhibition
TANK (Naritake Fukumoto,
    Ai Noguchi, Takashi Arai)
Takahiro Kai
Tsuguhiro Komazaki
Takashi Takamoto
Masayasu Fujiwara

**Exhibition Design
Management**
associates (Kozo Kadowaki,
    Akiko Kadowaki)

With the special Support of
Ishibashi Foundation

With the Support of
Stroog
JINS Holdings
Suikoukai Medical
    Corporation, Japan
KAMAWANU
Window Research Institute

In Collaboration with
under design
IWASAKI ELECTRIC
NBC Meshtec
KUMONOS Corporation
DAIKO ELECTRIC
Japan 3D Printer
HAGIHARA INDUSTRIES
    INC.
Rotho Blaas

Abnormal +, Peter Adey, Xenia Adjoubei, Christine Aglot, Ahn Eun-me, Ahn Jae Woo,
Ji Yoon Ahn, Ryu Ahn, Ahn Sang-soo, Arko Art Center, Arts Letters and Numbers
○ Namwoo Bae, Jaeha Ban, Catrina Beevor, Andrew Benjamin, Ana Betancour,
Joshua Bolchover, Lara Bober, Joff Bradley, Marco Bruno, Matthew Butcher ○
Simone Careno, Marcello Carpino, Pablo Castro, Hyunbae Chang, Kyuhyung Cho,
Cho Minsuk, Tony Cho, Young - Rong Choo, Binna Choi, Hyewon Choi, Sunwoong Choi,
Taeyoon Choi, Yunhee Choi, Jae Sung Chon, Choson Exchange, Calvin Chua, Harry Chun,
Alejandro Haiek Coll, Claudia Consonni, Maria Crispal, Gaia Crocella ○ Anshuman Dasgupta,
Jacopo David, Nick De Pace, Mark William Devenney, Killian Doherty ○ Oriana Eliçabe ○
Frida Foberg, Marialisa Fontanabona, Anthony Fontenot ○ G-Campus, Global Free Unit,
Marco Gambare, Chiara Garbin, David Gersten, Davide Giacometti, Emine Gorgul,
Antigoni Goutakoli, Rupali Gupte, H. Meltem Ö. Gürel ○ Nuri Han, Han Sungpil, Peter Hasdell,
HRS, Rhianon Morgan Hatch, Jason Hilgefort, Azuma Hiroki, Mingi Hong, Haobin Huang,
Doojin Hwang, Jie-Eun Hwang, Nahyun Hwang, Jeong Heon Hyeon ○ Mattia Inselvini,
Stella Ioannidou ○ Matt James, Sejeong Jang, YoungGyu Jang, Jinhong Jeon, Hyeyoon Jeong,
Jeong Mi sun, Dann Jessen, Kihyun Jo, Daeun Joo, Jungja Ju, Dongkoo Jung, Hyeyoon Jung,
Soyeon Jung ○ E Roon Kang, Youngmean Kang, Hanif Mohamed Kara, Amalia Katopodis,
Annie Kim, Ah-Yeon Kim, Daecheon Kim, Dongsei Kim, Eun Jeong Kim, Hansoo Kim,
Jae K. Kim, Jikyung Kim, Jin-Hyoung Kim, Jooyoung Kim, Jungyoon Kim, Kwangsoo Kim,
Kyunchul Kim, You Been Kim, So Young Kim, Sunhyun Kim, Taedong Kim, Taeyoon Kim,
Ted Kim, Hitomi Koyama ○ Andreas Lang, Andrew LeClair, Alex Taek-Gwang Lee, Aram Lee,
Changju Lee, Dong Yong Lee, Haevan Lee, Hyewon Lee, Hyunhee Lee, Jennifer Lee,
JiYun Lee, Jihoi Lee, Jinhye Lee, Jinhyoung Lee, Peter Lee, Sang-youp Lee, SeungEun Lee,
Sojin Lee, Taehyun Lee, Yong Ju Lee, Yoojin Lee, Leeon Architects, Ryan Leifield,
Christiano Lepratti, Yeonghwan Lim, Sojin Lee, Jade Keun Hye Lim, Soojung Lim, Xiaoxuan Lu,
Cristiano Luchetti, Rafael Luna, Peter Lynch ○ Joon Ma, Manoj NY, Leonidas Martin,
David Ortega Martinez, Davide Masserini, Corinne Mazzoli, Hasbrouck Miller, MiMi,
Amanda Monfrooe, Raffaele Marone, David Eugin Moon, Mospiran, Robert Mull, Kent Mundle,
○ NHDM Architects, Stankomir Nicieja, Carlotta Novella ○ ODÆRI, One-Aftr,
Ayselin Gozde Yildiz Oguzalp, Jooyoung Oh, Minwook Oh, Sang Hoon Oh, Eymen Özkan ○
Hyungmin Pai, Byungchul Park, Chung Whan Park, Daham Park, Donghee Park,
Dongmin Park, Jennifer Park, Kyong Park, Seongtae Park, Hyun Park, Lukas Pauer, PaTI,
Mark Pearce, Annie Pedret, Erik Persson, Giada Peterle, Luca Pili, Claudia Pochana,
Mateusz Pozar ○ Thomas Randall-Page, Gerard Reinmuth, Rhaomi, Chris Ro, Anne O Rourke,
Alessandro Russo, Haemin Ryu, Minjoo Ryu ○ Luigi Savio, David Sax, Christian Schweitzer,
Kelli Scott, Rafi Segal, Dong-jin Seo, Hyun-Suk Seo, Wontae Seo, Sewoon.School,
Prasad Shetty, Yoshiko Shimada, Youngkyu Shim, Hae Won Shin, Hyunjoon Shin, Inseop Shin,
Kyungmi Shin, Slow Signal, Leo James Smith, Hojun Song, Ryul Song, Seonghee Song,
Yehwan Song, Giuseppe Stampone, Studio 909A, Studios terra, Stuff Design, Yehre Suh,
Shawn Sullivan, Heidi Svenningsen-Kajita ○ Nader Tehrani, Dolf Jan Hendrik te Lintelo,
Ipek Türeli ○ Toshiya Ueno, Francesca Ulivi ○ Alexander Valentino, David Valldeby,
Carl-Johan Vesterlund ○ Ian Waelder, Maya West, Tobias Westerlund, Anna Winston ○
Myungsim Yang, Dowon Yi, Jaehee Yi, Dongwoo Yim, Junghyun Yoon, Jeongwon Youn,
Young Architects Forum Korea ○ Slavoj Žižek, Yoon Zo, Kyung Jin Zoh

Pavilion of Korea, 2021

70

Republic of Korea

FUTURE SCHOOL

Future School converts the Korean pavilion into an international incubator for radical thinking – a site for the exploration of ideas, knowledge, and projects that actively engage with the notion of building a positive future.

The exhibition area of the Korean pavilion is connected to a new digital environment and *Future School* campuses in Seoul and across the globe, facilitating generative dialogues and forging multiple solidarities through imaginative speculation around humanity's most pressing challenges.

Drawing on experimental educational practices, the pavilion overturns the concept of a school as a hierarchical institution, reframing it as a liminal space of exchange and connection, an evolving meeting place where participants can build community. Together with contributing architects, educators, artists, theorists, and advocates, participants are invited to engage in acts of unlearning and relearning through *Future School* events running throughout the 17th International Architecture Exhibition in Venice. These include workshops, roundtables, lectures, performances, and exhibitions in Venice and internationally, which will be collected and broadcast within the pavilion as part of an installation that will grow and change over time.

Visitors to the *Future School* in both its physical and virtual manifestations can participate in over fifty programmes exploring different issues, from cooling urban environments and the futurology of schools to innovative spatial interventions and borders as spaces of integration. With this extensive programme of conversations and actions, *Future School* becomes a catalyst for collaborative engagement on urgent topics. As a starting point to bring participants together, thought leaders and engaged citizens assembled around three critical, activating themes: diaspora, climate crisis, and innovation.

The aspiration to cultivate cross-disciplinary, interactive engagement of all kinds is reflected in the flexible use of the pavilion site – specifically the inclusion of informal domestic spaces that gently but resolutely dissolve the boundaries between learning and living. These include an open kitchen, a circular lounge, and a retreat room constructed entirely in hanji, a traditional, handmade Korean paper.

The Korean pavilion – *Future School* is also a founding member, together with other pavilions of this year's Architecture Biennale, of the Curators' Collective, which aims to foster international cooperation during a period of unprecedented change and global insecurity.

Commissioner
Arts Council Korea

Curator
Hae-Won Shin

Participants
Please refer to the Korean pavilion website to learn about the more than 300 *Future School* contributors www.korean-pavilion.or.kr

With the Support of
WOORIBANK
AMOREPACIFIC

Containporary, 2019-2020. Scale model

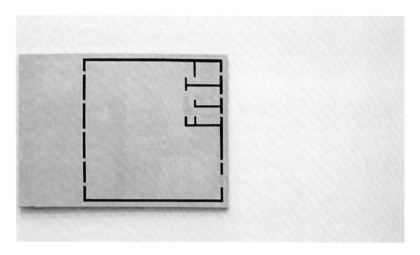

Pavilion K, 2018

Prishtina, 2017

Republic of Kosovo

CONTAINPORARY

Earth is Home

The role of urbanisation is to create sustainable environments that bring humanity and nature together, and that contribute to planetary biodiversity. This is the noblest mission of architecture. Global urbanisation is expanding, as can be seen from our unbridled population growth and the proliferation of megastructures (in the housing, economic, and communications fields and beyond). This means that every decision made by a country or society has a global impact, and a lack of sustainable planning places Earth even more at risk.

The most critical issue we face today is global warming, yet we lack the awareness and coordinated actions to avoid the almost certainly inevitable effects of climate disaster. Sustainable urbanisation must respect ecosystem balances.

Urb-Architecture uses an innovative approach to the construction of highly sustainable structures designed to protect the environment. Environmental 'shaping' revolutionises social, political, and spatial concepts as it strengthens connections between people and countries. Currently, megastructures are no guarantee of consistency – they have many stakeholders (governments, financial players, multinationals...) with sometimes conflicting interests, and all of these stakeholders have little consideration for rational planning and innovative use of existing resources.

But Earth and nature *are* transformable. Memory must be activated in the conscious world as an ideal, a fantastical world of opportunities that architects and planners renew and update.

Kosovo has for decades been 'developed' and degraded by dirty technology. This chapter must be closed, and sustainable development should begin now.
—MAKSUT VEZGISHI

Commissioner
Jehona Shyti,
Department of Culture,
Ministry of Culture

Curator
Maksut Vezgishi

Participants
Maksut Vezgishi
Vildane Maliqi
Argjirë Krasniqi
Feray Dervis
Recep Kerkezi
Gezim Radoniqi

Organisation
Ministry of Culture, Youth
and Sport of the Republic
of Kosovo

Design
Nita Salihu

Photographer
Edon Agushi

Music
Elvis and Gjulian Bytyqi

**Supportive-Consultative,
Research and Technical
Team**
Vildane Maliqi
Argjirë Krasniqi
Feray Dervis
Recep Kerkezi
Gezim Radoniqi

With the Support of
Presidency of the Republic
of Kosovo

All images: pavilion of Kuwait, 2020.
In collaboration with Atlas of Places

Kuwait

SPACE WARS

Commissioner
Zahra Ali Baba, Kuwait
  National Council for
  Culture Arts and Letters

Curators
Asaiel Al Saeed
Aseel Al Yaqoub
Saphiya Abu Al-Maati
Yousef Awaad

**Contributions and
Collaborations**
Abdullah AlGhunaim
Atlas of Places
Ayesha Kamal Khan
Aiysha Alsane
Bab.nimnim
Dani Ploeger
David Green
Faysal Tabbarah
Formless Finder
Jawad Altabtabai
LCLA Office
Abdulaziz AlJassim
Mohammed Alkouh
Maees Hadi
Nada Al Qallaf
Post Petroleum
Society Reem Alissa
Dana Alhasan
Samia Henni
Sara Alajmi
Sara Al-Ateeqi
Sijal Collective
Studio Toggle
The Open Workshop

Project Coordinators
Jaber Al Qallaf
Alaa Baroun

Administrative Support
Tahani Al-Adwani
Sultan AlDuweish

Art Direction
TB.D Studio

Commissioned by the National Council for Culture, Arts, and Letters, the Kuwait pavilion responds to the theme set forth, – *How will we live together?* through the discovery, interpretation, and projection of the hinterland. Oftentimes viewed as a counter to the forms that constitute the metropolitan, the surrounding and seemingly unoccupied landscape serves as the nation's functional staging ground through resource extraction, agricultural cultivation, military installations and cultural sedimentation. While necessary for the support and production that fund and logistically provide for the city-state, these landscapes remain isolated, both spatially and in discourse.

For Kuwait, the year 2021 marks the 70th anniversary of the first master plan commission and the 30th anniversary of the Gulf War (also known as the 'First Space War'). As we absorb the year, and the milestone it represents, new development plans are set that inform the expansion beyond the metropolitan – ultimately converging with the hinterland. As the radial city's imminent growth looms, the status of these spaces remains in question. Their competing functions and ambigous growth patterns, will inevitably lead to 'space wars' that compete for survival.

How will these spaces continue to exist next to, between, and amidst one another? Will their spatial territories surrender to the metropolitan's expansion campaign? The pavilion aims to address these questions in order to define the future of these spaces under threat – threat from extinction, overuse, domination, and, at times, the threat of being forgotten.

Kuwait's regional positioning has generated historical references through which the hinterland can be read and, at a scale vulnerable to analysis, allows it to be scrutinised. This year's approach positions Kuwait as a case study to understand these past, present, and future narratives. Thus, within a wider discourse, it offers itself as a test bed to expand the scope of the architect towards the hinterland. The curatorial direction comes in response to the interest of the National Council for Culture, Art and Letters to commission projects that engage with the cultural expressions and archaeological histories embodied in the desert landscape and the intelligence of land management inherited within what seems to be a priori of the urban form.

NRJA, *It's not for you! It's for the building*, 2021.
Exhibition visualisation by NRJA

NRJA, *It's not for you! It's for the building*, 2021.
Exhibition visualisation by NRJA

Latvia

IT'S NOT FOR YOU!
IT'S FOR THE BUILDING

With climate crisis at our doorstep, every architect now has an urgent global problem to solve. As crucial as technologies are in finding solutions, they also risk creating new problems along the way. Our exhibition and the accompanying book explore human resistance to technology as a pressing issue in contemporary architecture. By focusing on instances of unsettling techno-nonsense, we highlight the importance of the human perspective in architecture and stress the need to help people learn to live together with today's intelligent machines. In so doing, we pursue an informed and balanced coexistence of comfort-seeking individuals with sustainability-driven technology as the condition for a liveable future for humanity.

The Latvian pavilion installation focuses on the contradictory nature of our relationship with technology. Made of an uncanny web of black pipes from an unknown source, the enormous apparatus first appears to be a foreign organism parasitising space that used to belong to humans. The installation invites visitors to change their perspective and discover an amusing neighbour in this seemingly threatening intruder – one that reacts to our presence and even addresses us in an incomprehensible yet comforting language of its own. This immersive experience of learning to live with technology spells out a promise of a sustainable partnership between humans and machines, which are, after all, our own creations made for our own good – notwithstanding any initial negative sentiments.

The accompanying book elaborates on the idea behind the exhibition by confronting two opposite viewpoints on the role of technology in our everyday lives: satirical portrayals of absurd situations involving systems and equipment in the built environment on the one hand, the reasoned arguments of technology experts seeking to fix the problem on the other. Based on real-life cases, the short stories involve witty humour with techno-pessimist overtones, while expert commentaries display the dedicated pursuit of professionals believing in the ultimate good of technology. Thus, the book reflects the way our society, and often each one of us individually, is polarised towards the machines. It also shows that, in the long run, what may have seemed only 'for the building' proves to be 'for you' after all.
— LEVELUP

Commissioner
Jānis Dripe,
    Ministry of Culture
    of the Republic of
    Latvia

Curators
NRJA
(Uldis Lukševics,
Elina Libiete)

Participants
NRJA
(Uldis Lukševics,
Elina Libiete, Ivars
Veinbergs, Ieva Lāce-
Lukševica, Zigmārs
Jauja, Inga Dubinska,
Līga Jumburga)

Exhibition Concept
NRJA

Book Concept
NRJA
Levelup

**Exhibition
Realisation**
NRJA
Ansis Bergmanis
Pēteris Riekstiņš
Edgars Ošs
Mārtiņš Dāboliņš
Juris Simanovičs
Viesturs Laiviņš

Graphic Design
Aleksejs Muraško

Audio Design
Gatis Ziema

Video Design
Ēriks Božis

Project Management
Austra Bērziņa

Public Relations
Linda Bērziņa

With the Support of
Ministry of Culture
    of the Republic of
    Latvia

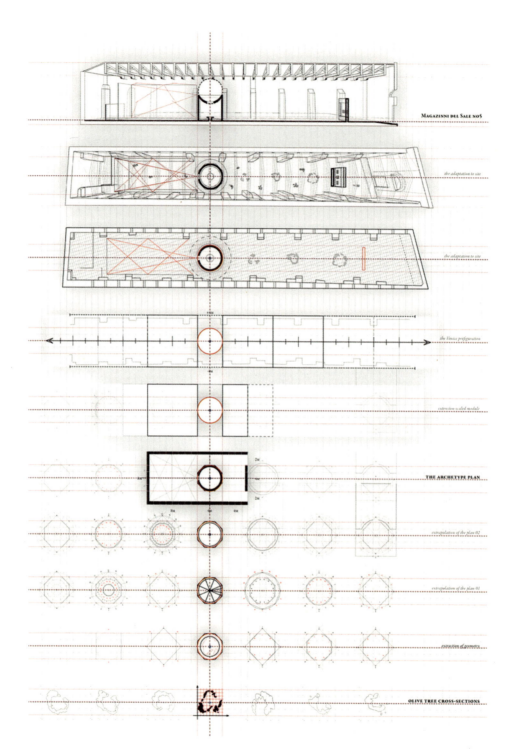

Magazzini del Sale no5

the adaptation to site

the adaptation to site

the Venice prefiguration

extrusion-scaled models

THE ARCHETYPE PLAN

extrapolation of the plan 02

extrapolation of the plan 01

extraction of geometry

OLIVE TREE CROSS-SECTIONS

Pavilion of Lebanon, Project Concept, HW architecture, 2021

Lebanon

A ROOF FOR SILENCE

A Roof for Silence evokes the theme of living together through the notion of emptiness as a necessary condition of architecture, as well as poetry, painting and music. A project that takes on its full and deepest meaning following the turbulences that occurred in Lebanon in the last year.

Born of a privileged collaboration with the poet and artist Etel Adnan, *A Roof for Silence* is designed around one of her seminal artworks and through the observation of a set of sixteen millennial olive trees in Lebanon's hinterland. Using mythological and contemporary references, the project brings together different eras and disciplines thanks to the participation of both Lebanese and French artists, such as Paul Virilio, Alain Fleischer and Fouad Elkoury. More than an architectural project, *A Roof for Silence* is a manifesto for a new form of architecture that restores the importance of the void and of silence.

The installation is introduced by the 'anti-form' paintings of Paul Virilio, who saw emptiness as the depth of time. Virilio's works resonate with photogrammetric scans taken from inside the hollow trunks of the olive trees – explorations of absent matter that draw us into the architectural space. A triptych video-projection of the trees of Lebanon, filmed in the obscurity of the night, prolongs our immersion in the theme.

A Roof for Silence hinges on a central construction designed to house a work by Etel Adnan that consists of a set of paintings entitled *Olivéa: Hommage à la déesse de l'olivier*. These sixteen paintings form a cycle, like a single poem. Adnan doesn't represent specific olive trees, but the feeling inspired in her by a genus of tree that has been part of all Mediterranean civilisations, far outstripping our limited human lives.

Commissioner
Jad Tabet

Curator
Hala Wardé

Participants
Etel Adnan
Fouad Elkoury
Paul Virilio
Alain Fleischer

Contributors
Centre Pompidou
Galerie Lelong
Le Fresnoy
Soundwalk collective
Bits to Atoms

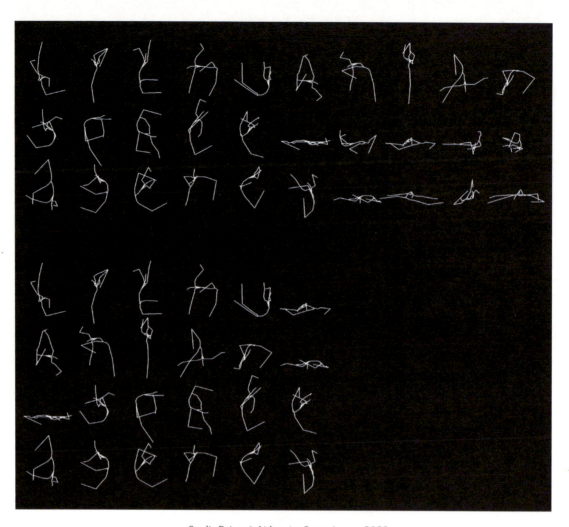

Studio Pointer®, *Lithuanian Space Agency*, 2020.
Corporate identity, custom programmed typeface based on the human skeleton.
© Lithuanian Space Agency, Julijonas Urbonas, Studio Pointer®

Julijonas Urbonas, *Planet of People*, 2019, 3D astrophysics simulation.
© Lithuanian Space Agency, Julijonas Urbonas, Studio Pointer®

Lithuania

LITHUANIAN SPACE AGENCY PRESENTS PLANET OF PEOPLE

The Lithuanian Space Agency (LSA) is an organisation researching cosmic architecture and gravitational aesthetics. The LSA presents Julijonas Urbonas' *Planet of People* - an artistic and scientific study into a hypothetical artificial planet made up of human bodies.

Instead of sending humans to colonise other planets, what if we catapulted them into a specific location in outer space - free of gravity, light and air - to form a new planet, a planet of people?

The LSA presents a prototype to test this out and explores what it would actually take to create such a planet. Employing expertise from a wide range of disciplines, including space architecture, astroart, space engineering, astroethics, astroanthropology, astrobiology and astrophysics, the LSA raises questions about the potential aesthetic, ethical and political implications of realising *Planet of People*. The agency proposes to take on *Planet of People* as an extraterrestrial perspective towards our current and future life on Earth and beyond.

Along with these interdisciplinary feasibility studies, *Planet of People* also uses a 3D scanner to scan the participants of the experiment and 'send' them into space as animated simulations based on planetary science. As more and more people participate over the course of the trial run in Venice, their scanned, irregularly dispersed, levitating bodies will be drawn to each other due to their weak gravities and clump together, thereby forming a new celestial body.

The project opens up the cosmic imagination of architecture and expands our thinking about life in outer space beyond artificial gravity stations and geodesic space colonies, among many other similar space constructs. The LSA functions as a platform for conversations revolving around topics such as astroaesthetics, eschatological imagination, astroanthropocene, extraterrestrial anthropocentrism, terraforming and the inversion of Vitruvian architecture.

Alongside the main installation, the LSA introduces other projects and their prototypes by Urbonas that investigate a range of historical references to gravitational aesthetics and explore how gravity shapes human life, thought, and imagination.

Commissioner
Julija Reklaitė, Rupert

Curator
Jan Boelen

Participant
Julijonas Urbonas

....

Assistant Curator
Milda Batakytė

Laboratory Design
Isora x Lozuraityte
    Studio

**Deployable
Structures Design**
Vladas Suncovas

Engineering
Povilas Ambrasas

Graphic Design
Studio Pointer°

Programming
Studio Pointer°
Fred Rodrigues

Producer
Mindaugas Reklaitis

Communication
Jogintė Bučinskaitė
Vilius Balčiūnas

Local Manager
Marco Scurati

Coordinators
Eglė Kliučinskaitė
Erika Urbelevič

Presented by
Lithuanian Council
    for Culture

Organised by
Rupert - centre for
    art, residencies and
    education

Strategic Partner
X Museum, Beijing

Partners
Gallery Vartai, Vilnius
Gioielli Nascosti di
    Venezia
Collective, City
    Observatory,
    Edinburgh
National Gallery of
    Art, Vilnius
Plasta
Science Gallery,
    Dublin
15min

Collaborators
Formuniform
Kosmica Institute
Lithuanian Aerospace
    Association
Lithuanian Culture
    Institute
Vilnius Academy of
    Arts
Vilnius City
    Municipality
Vilnius Tech, Faculty
    of Architecture
Vilnius University

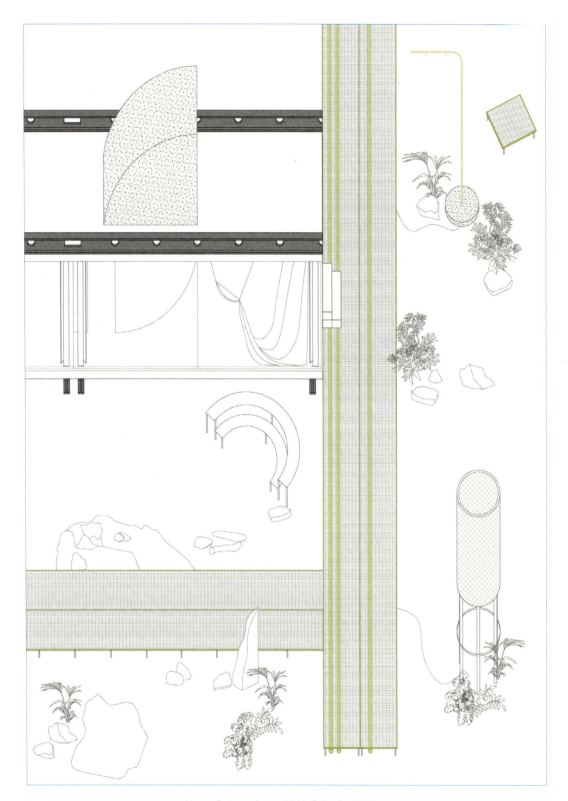

Homes for Luxembourg, 2021. © Studio SNCDA

Grand Duchy of Luxembourg

HOMES FOR LUXEMBOURG

The first pandemic of the Anthropocene hardly left a stone unturned. Where decades of promoting the concept of sustainability failed, the spreading virus succeeded in the wink of an eye. The collective experience of being catapulted into a way of living within a limited radius, minimal contacts, and reduced consumption provoked a dramatic shakeup of mindsets. It set a spotlight on the relationship between architecture and land, urban and rural, interior and exterior, home and work/study, built environment and nature.

Referring to the official motto of this year's Biennale, *How will we live together?*, the Luxembourg contribution to the 17th International Architecture Biennale comes with an exhibition that reflects on these dualities. The modular installation in the Sale d'Armi and several contributions to the architecture magazine 'Accattone' explore ways of reversible living, offering a vision for a model of repurposing land as new urban commons, providing new forms of togetherness. The contributors to this exhibition come from diverse disciplines, and include architects, artists, authors, urban planners, photographers, ecologists, developers, lawyers...

The pavilion hosts working spaces for the participants of Luxembourg's first ever curatorial residency programme at the Biennale di Venezia. Emerging curators, authors, mediators, scenographers, bloggers, and activists in the field of architecture have the possibility to explore this year's Architecture Biennale, get a first-hand overview of the current state of international discourse, gain a deeper understanding of the challenges and opportunities of contributing to the world's most important architecture exhibition, enhance their professional abilities, and establish important contacts and develop ideas for own projects.

Commissioner
Ministry of Culture, Luxembourg

Curator
LUCA Luxembourg Center for Architecture

Participants
Studio SNCDA
Koenraad Dedobbeleer
Martine Feipel & Jean Bechameil

Delegated Exhibition Curator
Sara Noel Costa de Araujo (Studio SNCDA)

Organiser
LUCA Luxembourg Center for Architecture (Andrea Rumpf)

Cultural Programming and Emerging Talent Program
LUCA Luxembourg Center for Architecture

Exhibition Architecture
Studio SNCDA (LU/BE)

Photography
Valentin Bansac
Eric Chenal

Structural Engineers
Bollinger + Grohmann

Website Design
Studio Michel Welfringer

Construction
Christoph Van Damme

Publication
Accattone, Issue 7, May 2021
Editors: Sophie Dars, Carlo Menon, Galaad Van Daele
Designers: Ismael Bennani + Orphée Grandhomme (Überknackig)

Team
LUCA Luxembourg Center for Architecture (Andrea Rumpf, Director; Thomas Miller, Giulia Zatti, Eline Bleser, Pascale Kauffman, Alvise Pagnacco)
Studio SNCDA (Sara Noel Costa de Araujo, Valentin Bansac, Lisa Brugière, Ester Goris, Arnaud Hendrickx)

Financed by
Ministry of Culture, Luxembourg

LUCA is supported by
Ministry of Culture
Œuvre Nationale de Secours Grande-Duchesse Charlotte
OAI Ordre des Architectes et des Ingénieurs-Conseils
Banque de Luxembourg
Prefalux
Soludec
A+P Kieffer
OMNITEC
Annen
ENOVOS Luxembourg
EQUITONE
Geberit b.v. Luxembourg
JUNG
Karp-Kneip Constructions
La Luxembourgeoise
Minusines
OST Fenster
Paul Wurth
S+B Inbau
Schüco International
Socom
Tarkett
VELUX Commercial

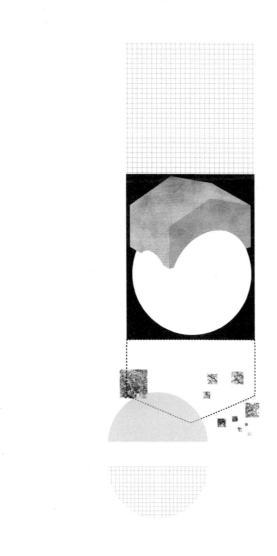

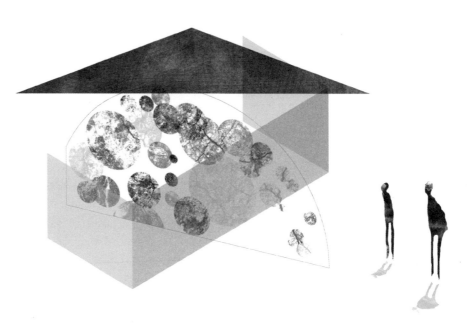

All images: *Now*, pavilion of the Republic of North Macedonia, 2021

Republic of North Macedonia
NOW

Commissioner
Dita Starova Kjerimi,
National Gallery
of the Republic
of North Macedonia

Curators
Bekir Ademi
Jordan Šišovski

Participants
Bekir Ademi
Jordan Šišovski
Ana Rafailovska
Amine Ademi
Enis Abovski
Atanas Naumovski
Enes Sever
Dren Nevzati
Gavril Boshkovski
Elmedina Hasani
Nita Çavolli
Aida Bakalli Salihu
Ivana Chaloska

Organisation
BINA (Bureau of Inventive
    Architecture)

Collaborators
Ferid Muhić
Ramush Muarem

With the Support of
Ministry of Culture
of the Republic of North
    Macedonia

Negotiating *Now*

Now – an imaginary interval mediating past and future, loaded with uncertainty, fuelled by utopian hopes. The ephemerality of this interval often reveals utopian hopes all too easily realised in dystopian grievances, as in the case with architectural utopia(s) of the avantgarde. Furthermore, Modernism raised the bar far too high for architecture to make a better world, while Postmodernism lowered the bar far too low, in a flux of past and present hypes – AI, automation, the fourth industrial revolution, post-digital aesthetics – all competing to be the bearers of a new paradigm shift. Will this new paradigm embody our hopes for the future, or our fears? Or something completely different?

Meditating *Now*

What does architecture mean today? Is architecture other people? The porosity at the core of our project aims at opening us up to a meditation on these questions. It opens our gaze up to the Sky, to the Open, but in doing so it brings our gaze back to ourselves as well as to the inability to escape the ever-present gaze of everyone around us. We see the Sky, the unconcealed, but also the Earth, the concealed. Is our Ground the Earth or the Sky? To deal with these questions we need to contemplate the origins of architecture. Instead of calculative thinking, we have to be open to meditative thinking. We have to stand firmly on the Ground, but be open to the Sky.

Captivating *Now*

The allusion to Plato's cave calls forth not only each of us personally to rethink our relation to truth, but also our culture, our civilisation, as well as our architectural profession. Are we not also prisoners of our prejudices? Are not our 'self-evident truths' just shadows on the wall of our close-mindedness and hubris? Are we not prisoners of our nations, religions, ideologies, identities, and class interests? Should we not strive for more openness and more porousness of the walls of our ignorance? Are we not also, as architects, prisoners to ideas and values, which are just a shadow of the truth? How should the architect respond to the trend of designing modern Plato's caves? Should she help in the further imprisonment of the captives?

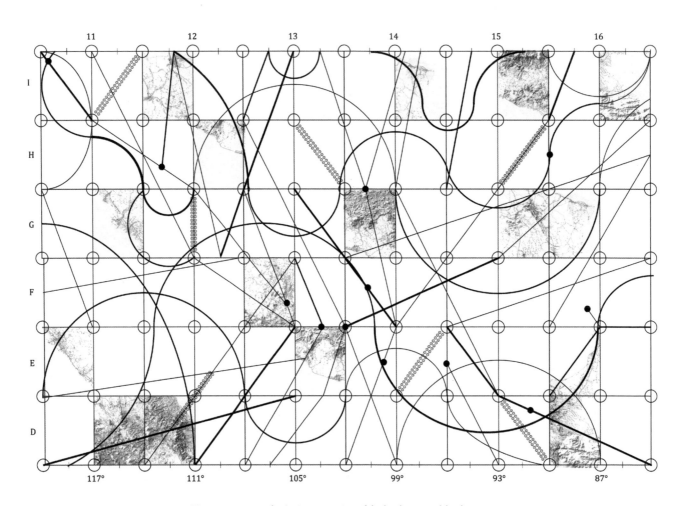

Uncommon grounds: An interpretation of the landscapes of displacement
in Mexican territory. The grid of the UTM (Universal Transverse Mercator)
projection system denotes the tension between the local particulars
and the homogenising forces of global logics

Mexico

DISPLACEMENTS /
DESPLAZAMIENTOS

Mexico, due to its geological and geographical condition, is positioned as one of the megadiverse countries of the world and a multicultural rich territory. However, we have excluded social and natural systems from our territorial management practices.

Neoliberalism has promoted conditions of dispossession and displacement of vulnerable populations and ecosystems, increased inequality, and environmental crisis. Architecture, to a great extent, has been at the service of this political economy.

Mexico's pavilion seeks to reflect on 'displacements', as a result of evident inequality, environmental degradation, risk vulnerability, and violence. The pavilion focuses on the architects' ability to recognise, observe, and analyse the role of collective organisation, as an emergent condition that has allowed groups to survive with few resources, by means of adaptation, self-organisation, and anti-fragility capacities when faced with forces of displacement.

The design of the pavilion is based on a collective curatorial creative process as a laboratory. The curatorship is undertaken by a team instead of a single curator; and twelve participants. This approach attempts to break with conventional structures of knowledge and action, whether binary, heteronormative, colonial, or anthropocentric. It is constituted by a critical exercise in conjunction with a material and spatial exploration, defined by a dialogue between the curators and participants that eschews authorship, where successive collective fragmentary iterations build a (tentative) totality.

Our goal is to situate architecture in relation to social and environmental displacements that characterise our territory, and that have remained largely ignored by design practices. The pavilion, as the spatial and experiential result of our inquiries, questions how to design and build spaces of belonging, reconciliation, storytelling, exchange, recovery, assimilation, forgiveness, and resistance in the context of displacement.

—NATALIA DE LA ROSA, ISADORA HASTINGS, MAURICIO ROCHA, AND ELENA TUDELA

Commissioner
Gabriela Gil
    Verenzuela

Curators
Natalia de la Rosa
Isadora Hastings
Mauricio Rocha
Elena Tudela

Participants
Antonio Plá Pérez
Fernanda Canales
Gabriel Konzevik
    Cabib
Judith Meléndrez
    Bayardo
Sandra Calvo
Rosario Hernández
    Arguello
Rozana Montiel
Escobedo Solíz
    Arquitectos
    (Andrés Solíz Paz,
    Pavel Escobedo)
Estudio MMX (Jorge
    Arvizu, Ignacio
    del Río, Emmanuel
    Ramírez, Diego
    Ricalde)
Estudio Macias Peredo
    (Magui Peredo,
    Salvador Macias,
    Diego Quirarte)
Estudio Nuñez Zapata
    (Roberto Nuñez,
    Katia Zapata)
OH Abogados (Juan
    Ó Gorman, Pablo
    Gutiérrez de la
    Peza)
JC Arquitectura (Juan
    Carral)
Kiltro Polaris (Victor
    Ebergenyi Kelly)
PLUG Architecture
    (Román Cordero
    Tovar, Izbeth
    Mendoza)
Taller de Proyectos

Incidencia
Regenerativa de
la Universidad
Iberoamericana
CDMX (Juan
Casillas Pintor,
Roberto Contreras,
Adrian Sánchez)

Organisation
Alejandra Frausto,
    Minister of Culture
    of Mexico
Lucina Jiménez,
    General Director of
    Instituto Nacional
    de Bellas Artes y
    Literatura

Vasilija Abramović, Ruairi Glynn, Parker Heyl,
Syntony – motion room, 2020

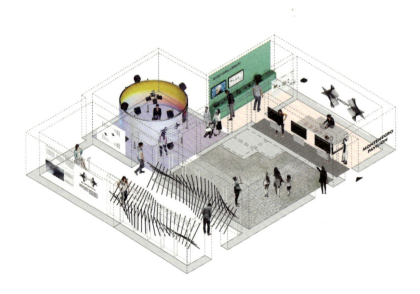

Vasilija Abramović, Ruairi Glynn, Parker Heyl,
Syntony - isometric drawing, 2020

Montenegro

MONTENEGRO WITHDREW ITS
PARTICIPATION WHILE THE CURRENT
VOLUME WAS BEING PRINTED

SYNTONY BY VASILIJA ABRAMOVIĆ, RUAIRI GLYNN AND PARKER HEYL

Commissioner
Dragan Vuković

Curator
Svetlana K. Perović

Participants
Svetlana K. Perović
Vasilija Abramović
Ruairi Glynn
Parker Heyl

Collaborators
Stephen Gage
    (Architectural
    Researcher)
Gabriella Vigliocco
    (Experimental
    Psychologist)
Fiona Zisch
    (Neuroscientist
    and Architectural
    Researcher)
Florin Gheorghiu
    (Neuroscientist)
Gonçalo Lopes
    (Software Engineer
    and Neuroscientist)
Sarah Rubidge
    (Choreographer)
Sam McElhinney
    (Architect and
    Researcher in
    Spatial Perception)
Kongpyung Moon
    (Creative
    Technologist)
Luca Delatorre
    (Acoustics
    Engineer)
Francesco Anselmo
    (Lighting
    Engineering)
Dominik Zisch
    (Computer
    Scientist)
Paul Bavister (Sound
    Designer and
    Bio-Sensing
Researcher);
Miljana Zeković
    (Architectural
    Researcher)
Milena Vukčević,
    Iva Milošević,
    Marija Ćaćić,
    Saria Ghaziri
    (Architects)
Francesco Paolo
    Lamacchia (Civil
    Engineer)
Dalia Todary-Michael
    (Landscape
    Designer)
Peng Gao (Creative
    Technologist)

With the Support of
Interactive
    Architecture Lab,
    The Bartlett School
    of Architecture,
    University College
    London
BMade

The word *syntony* comes from the Greek *syn* meaning 'together' and *tonos* meaning 'tone' or 'voice'. *Syntony* is a phenomenon of resonance where multiple waveform frequencies come together in harmony. It is also a social concept. The emergence of paradigms, or a Zeitgeist, are cases of cultural *syntony*, a new coming together of ideas and techniques.

Montenegro's participation in the 17th International Architecture Exhibition is theoretically framed – *Towards a Transactive Spatial Perception* – by the national pavilion curator Svetlana K. Perović in keeping with the director Sarkis' topic. In response to Svetlana K. Perović's call to stage an 'experiment' and contribute to the central theme of *How will we live together?*, the team's response is, in a word, 'transdisciplinarity'. They argue that architecture has a tendency towards acts of 'disciplinary imperialism', taking subject matter and methodologies from other fields of knowledge, separating them from their own discursive contexts, and superficially adopting features whose potency is reduced. These acts undermine the potential for architecture to be a productive holistic space for arts and sciences to live and work together. To achieve deeper, more meaningful and productive transactions they raise the question of how architecture should position itself and function within the ecology of disciplines.

The conceptual formulation of *Syntony* implies a broad coalition of art, architecture, science, and engineering. It includes collaborators from the neurosciences, psychology, computing, robotics, lighting, and acoustics using the visual metaphor of overlapping waveforms to symbolise the interaction and transaction of disciplinary fields. *Syntony* consists of a series of transdisciplinary laboratories where spatial perception experiments through motion, light, and sound can be explored interactively by visitors. Each lab environment consists of an automated sensing system that collects occupant data and interactively controls waveforms throughout the space. This includes an interactive kinetic installation able to manifest multiple simultaneous perceptual illusions of waves travelling through the gallery.
—VASILIJA ABRAMOVIĆ, RUAIRI GLYNN, PARKER HEYL

Red List Pond at the outdoor studio of Debra Solomon/Urbaniahoeve, 2020.
Photo Johannes Schwartz

Amsterdam Zuidoost Food Forest (VBAZO), Urbaniahoeve (Debra Solomon
& Renate Nollen) and the VBAZO Community of Practice, 2020
Photo Johannes Schwartz

Afaina de Jong and Innavisions, *Space of Other*, 2019.
Printed fabric, 5×3×4 m ca.
Courtesy Wozen Studio, Lisbon© CX Casulo

The Netherlands

WHO IS WE?

Het Nieuwe Instituut responds to the theme *How will we live together?* with the counter-question 'Who is we?'. The word 'we' seems to imply inclusion, but it often represents a very singular perspective that undermines the other. As social and ecological urgencies demand immediate care and action, it is fundamental that 'we' becomes an even more pluralised pronoun. 'We' should encompass all humans and non-humans such as soil, plants, animals, and microbes. While this position should guide all human behaviour, the presentation *Who is We?* addresses the urgency for architects and urbanists to commit to this plurality.

    Who is We? presents an urbanism that is female, indigenous, of colour, queer, and multispecies. It advocates for design values transforming the current – mostly exploitative – dynamic into equal and non-extractive forms of coexistence. The knowledge, values, and tools necessary for this transformation have been developed throughout history but are ignored by the architecture canon.

    In Venice and the Netherlands, *Who is We?* offers live encounters and digital reflections from various disciplines and collaborators. Contributors architect Afaina de Jong and artist Debra Solomon deconstruct normative concepts of space such as *terra nullius* and *tabula rasa*, visualising what remains unseen behind the dominant structures that define spaces.

    In *Multiplicity of Other,* De Jong reconstitutes the dominance of a single-sided universal minority perspective on cities, identifying the spatial knowledge of the overwhelming majority of othered groups as fundamental. She presents *Space of Other,* a performative space using public dialogues to engage with other values, languages, and spatial practices such as dance, music, and poetry. Solomon advocates *Multispecies Urbanism* for just urban development driven by reciprocal inter-species relations of care and climate crisis mitigation. In the pavilion she shares research tools such as Radical Observation, soil chromatograms, and rhizotrons to produce environmentally democratic urban landscapes in the form of public space food forests.

    Who is We? is an empathic plea against homogeneity as polyphony and plurality create the relations and interactions essential to build resilient societies and cities.
— FRANCIEN VAN WESTRENEN

Commissioner
Guus Beumer
Het Nieuwe Instituut

Curator
Francien van Westrenen
Het Nieuwe Instituut

Participants
Afaina de Jong
Debra Solomon

Graphic Design
Richard Niessen

**Collaborators
and Contributors**
Paul 'Seiji' Dolby
Juan Arturo García
Innavisions
Johannes Schwartz
Maia Kenney
Urbaniahoeve
   Foundation
VBAZO Community of
   Praxis
We Are Here Venice

Organisation
Het Nieuwe Instituut

Programme

Values for Survival
Caroline Nevejan, CSO
   City of Amsterdam
Huda AbiFarès, Khatt
   Foundation

*The Polder of Babel. A
   Superdiverse City in
   the Anthropocene*
Independent School for
   the City, Rotterdam

Affiliated research
Lada Hršak, Bureau
   LADA
Chiara Dorbolò and

Daphne Bakker,
   Failed Architecture
Tymon Hogenelst and
   Jesse van der Ploeg,
   Studio Wild

**International
Communication**
ING Media

With the Support of
Dutch Ministry of
   Education, Culture
   and Science
City of Amsterdam
City of Rotterdam
Creative Industries
   Fund NL
Embassy and Consulate
   General of the
   Kingdom of the
   Netherlands in Italy
Felix Meritis

Website
whoiswe.hetnieuwe-
   instituut.nl

Helen & Hard, *What We Share*, March 2020. Interior study.
Rendering © Helen & Hard; Nasjonalmuseet

Helen & Hard, *Workshop with residents, Stavanger*, 2019.
Video still, film photography Annar Bjørgli © Nasjonalmuseet

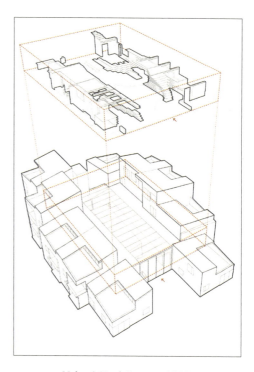

Helen & Hard, *Program*, 2020.
Digital drawing © Helen & Hard; Nasjonalmuseet

Nordic Countries
Norway-Sweden-Finland

WHAT WE SHARE.
A MODEL
FOR COHOUSING

The exhibition *What We Share* is a full-scale section of a prospective cohousing project. Here, Norwegian architects Helen & Hard have invited eight residents to share elements of their private life with each other and with the public. The installation serves as a model for how to build a community and a sustainable living environment simultaneously. The exhibition also includes a new video work by the artist Anna Ihle, who explores the political and economic dimensions of cohousing.

Commissioners
Stina Högkvist,
    The National Museum of
    Norway
Carina Jaatinen,
    Museum of Finnish
    Architecture, MFA
Kieran Long,
    ArkDes, Swedish National
    Centre for Architecture and
    Design

Curator
Martin Braathen,
    The National Museum
    of Norway

Participants
Helen & Hard Architects
Anna Ihle

In their ongoing work, Helen & Hard seek to challenge and modify the commercial housing sector in the Nordic region. By combining new communal solutions (40% of all Nordic households are single-person households) with home ownership (77% of Norwegians own their own homes), they are developing new, sustainable housing models where the inhabitants are active shareholders.

In Vindmøllebakken, a cohousing project designed by Helen & Hard in Stavanger, Norway, residents have fully equipped apartments with many shared facilities and spaces, and a vibrant local democracy. At the Nordic Pavilion in Venice, Helen & Hard continue their work with the residents of Vindmøllebakken, challenging them to further develop the idea of sharing as a key to communal living. Which functions and situations of their individual apartments are they willing to move out and share with others? These elements are introduced in a new interface between apartments and communal space – the semi-public sharing zone.

The history of collective living ranges between various extremes, from large, rationally organised communes to small, poetic cohabitation projects; from religiously or politically motivated utopias to the pre-War family hotels (which supported the liberation of women) and various radical alternatives to existing societal norms. In the 1970s, the Nordic model of cohousing was introduced as a pragmatic alternative, combining individual living units, shared spaces, self-ownership and community. The model has since spread across the globe, and forms the base for Helen & Hard new cohousing experiments.

While encouraging active participation and co-ownership, the housing project in *What We Share* hence belongs among the non-utopian end of the co-living spectrum. It is based on a commercial housing model, but relies on collaborative processes and close dialogue between architects, developers and residents. It implements a sustainable, flexible, open-source solid-timber construction system.

— MARTIN BRAATHEN

Ghora Ghari, *Horse Carriage, Mapping Festivities*, 2020.
© Sara M. Anwar

Shadi Hall facade, *Mapping Festivities*, 2020.
© Sara M. Anwar

Shadi Hall interior, *Mapping Festivities*, 2020.
© Sara M. Anwar

Pakistan

MAPPING FESTIVITIES

Mapping Festivities explores the many dimensions of weddings in Pakistan, as festive events that are both rich expressions of our cultural traditions and institutions that have a significant impact both at the social and urban level.

Mapping Festivities investigates weddings as events that create a spatial network; bringing together individuals and industries from diverse contexts and across all classes of society.

Acting as a *connective urban and territorial tissue*, these festivities are systems that *allow us to live together*. In contemporary Pakistan, weddings knit together a multiplicity of cultural, and economic interplays that are performed in high energy theatres of celebration. They open up a space for people from different industries and social classes to coexist in harmony. Our project particularly reveals the complex community that builds this underlying infrastructure, a community made up of architects, construction workers, designers, caterers, photographers, technicians, makeup artists, videographers, and performers. These people are the ordinary citizens that become purveyors of festive dreams.

Mapping Festivities studies the explicit typology of the wedding venue as a site for cultural production. The Shadi Hall first appeared in the early 1980s to address the needs of the fast-growing immigrant population of the city of Karachi. Residential villas were transformed into designated spaces for weddings through interventions such as the addition of a billboard-inspired entrance façade. This façade, physically and metaphorically, created a permeable boundary between the space of the city and a 'new' space for 'performance'. The Shadi Hall emerged as a direct response to the social and urban needs for a specific space to serve the wedding performance; a unique architectural typology born out of post-Partition, postcolonial Pakistan.
— SARA M. ANWAR

Commissioner
Kalim A. Siddiqui,
   Pakistan Council
   of Architects and
   Town Planners

Curator
Sara M. Anwar

Participants
Sara M. Anwar
Madeeha Yasin
   Merchant
Farhan Anwar
Shama Dossa
Hira Zuberi

Research Director
Madeeha Yasin
   Merchant

Lead Researcher
Farhan Anwar

Research Partner
Habib University

Advisor
Andrea Simitch

Content Advisor
Eric Baldwin

Exhibition
Consultant
Blanca Corbi

Coordinator, PCATP
Rashid Rasheed

Organisation
Laure Parise,
Najeh Zimmerman
   (Antidote art.
   design)

Production Team
Nabla Yahya
Syed Bahroz Ali

With the Support of
Pehchan Pakistan
Signtrade
Seltrade
ARCHITECTEM
Yasin and Zeenat
   Merchant
Firdaus Mohammad
   Anwar and Adnan
   Anwar Khokhar
Sara Bashir

Street Gate, 2019.
Photo Camila Villa Novoa.
Courtesy Patronato Cultural del Perú

Peruvian Pavilion Entry View, 2020.
Render Courtesy V. Oid

Peruvian Pavilion Interior View, 2020.
Render Courtesy V. Oid

Peru

PLAYGROUND: ARTEFACTS FOR INTERACTION

We respond to the prompt —*How will we live together?*— with an action/reflection, by using a local problem to take on a global challenge.

Our project removes gates/fences from public spaces in various districts of Lima and of Peru, to transform them into artefacts that invite people to interaction. These 'security' elements *cum* segregation devices are thus turned into benches, playground games, soccer goals, and so forth, in an effort to re-channel all of the time, money, and energy, expended into building barriers by breathing new life and meaning into their wrought materials.

Peru is still recovering from the scars of an internal conflict that raged from 1980 to 2000. The people of Lima started gating their streets as a defence mechanism. More than twenty years later, we have yet to stop gating ourselves. Like the rest of the world – given the new urban densities we are learning to live with, and faced with the persistency of the media and the precariousness of global politics, and now challenged by the new world order that is taking shape through the pandemic – we are becoming wary of each other once again. This situation could further exacerbate fear of one another and increase atomisation. Gates reify our fears, and we need to work on ways to transform those fears into opportunities.

Because of the pandemic, the pavilion is closed with an entry gate. The central artefacts of the exhibition are presented as a playground, the purpose of which is to invite us to interact with each other, to re-learn – through games for young and old alike – that we can generate new social contracts. Some of these artefacts are, for example, rocker benches that require another person as a counterweight for comfortable use.

Lenticular panels are hanged on the entry gate, where two versions of the same photograph —with and without gates— coexist. Through the lenticular film and depending on the visitor's movement, the gated photographs disappear into emblematic spaces clear of them. From local, physical gates, we then move on to less obvious and global ones.

The pavilion helps the visitor to reflect on what is left inside and out when gates are in the middle. After the exhibition, the playground artefacts will be returned to their original sites, for continuing transformation.

—FELIPE FERRER

Commissioner
José Orrego Herrera

Curator
Felipe Ferrer

Design Team
Javier Vásquez
Alejandro Alarcón
Luis Arévalo
Kevin Abanto
Erick Maldonado
Francisco Obregón
Daniela Díaz Tenorio
Marina Gubbins

Production
Patronato Cultural del Perú

In Collaboration with
CREA, Universidad de Lima
Servimetales
Moisés Salas
José Salas
Máximo Hinojosa
Maycol Ovalle

Graphic Design
Formato Público
(Michael Prado, Camila Villa, Elías Quiroz)

Collaborator
Mónica Belevan

Management and Coordination
eiletz ortigas | architects

Under the Auspices of
Fundación Wiese / El Comercio

With the Support of
PromPerú
Ministry of Foreign Trade and Tourism
Ministry of Culture
Ministry of Foreign Affairs
Universidad de Lima
Pontificia Universidad Católica del Perú
Universidad Nacional de Ingeniería
Universidad Privada del Norte
Municipalidad de Huamanga
Municipalidad de Pueblo Libre
Municipalidad de La Molina
Ascensores Powertech Lima, Cómo Vamos

With the additional Support of
ARTCO
Hunter Douglas
Decor Center
Trazzo Iguzzini
Marx Peru Center
Peruvian Architecture Firms Association – AEA

Lifting the first rafter, 2020.
Photo Alexander Eriksson Furunes

Structural frames on site, 2020.
Photo Alexander Eriksson Furunes

Testing the section in full scale, 2020.
Photo Ron Stephen Reyes

Philippines

STRUCTURES OF MUTUAL SUPPORT

Throughout history, traditions and strategies of mutual support have enabled communities to live together in the face of adversities and crises. People have come together to achieve a common goal through a process built on social relationships, reciprocity, and communal solidarity. *Bayanihan, Dugnad, Talkoot, Meitheal, Mutirão, Gotong-Royong*, and *Tequio* are different names around the world for this tradition. It has been a way to cope with tasks that go beyond the skills of an individual to farm, to construct, or to organise celebrations. However, such structures of resilience, self-organisation and collaboration are slipping away in current society where the currency of wealth is measured by money rather than the relationships we build among ourselves.

The exhibition is an open invitation for a dialogue to re-imagine architecture, broadly conceived, through structures of mutual support and how we value social and environmental resources that shape our built environment.

This inspires a renewed attentiveness to the hierarchies of knowledges, cultures, and values that we work with and how they are embedded in, and emerge from, whatever it is that we build together. Communities and architects alike are called to rethink the status quo or the state of norms, to learn from each other, and to act on a collectively negotiated common vision.

Structures of Mutual Support explores the Philippine imagination of *Bayanihan* and the Norwegian *Dugnad* as guiding principles for architectural praxis in an attempt to understand the implications of re-engaging with such traditions and strategies in contemporary time. Through a close collaboration over four months between the community of GK Enchanted Farm and the two architects Sudarshan V. Khadka Jr. and Alexander Eriksson Furunes, the group formed Framework Collaborative to explore the implications of planning, designing, and constructing a library and a *tambayan*, a space to hang out in, within the community. After three months of construction, the library was taken down and shipped to Venice to be exhibited as the Philippine pavilion. After the 17th International Architecture Exhibition, it will return home to the village.

Commissioner
National Commission for
    Culture and the Arts
    (NCCA)
Arsenio 'Nick' Lizaso

Curators and Participants
Framework Collaborative
(GK Enchanted Farm
    Community, Sudarshan V.
    Khadka Jr. and Alexander
    Eriksson Furunes)

Cooperating Agencies
Department of Foreign Affairs
Office of Congresswoman
    and Deputy Speaker Loren
    Legarda

All images: *Territory*, 2019. *Trouble in Paradise* research archive.
Photo Paweł Starzec. Courtesy Zachęta — National Gallery of Art

Poland

TROUBLE IN PARADISE

The exhibition recognises the countryside as an independent object of research, a product of states' explicit social and spatial experiments. It is here, outside of the city, that we seek answers to the question *How will we live together?*

The project in general focuses on the European post-socialist countryside, and in particular on the case of Poland – a country where 93% of the area is considered as rural.

In the context of an ongoing climate crisis, an internal migration towards the countryside, a constant housing shortage, and a problematic planning legislation, we must shift the debate towards the rural, look there for possible solutions and opportunities through a reintroduction of the idea of commons.

The exhibition is centred around an attempt to instrumentalise the history of forms of living, labour, and commoning in the countryside. Their interrelation is crucial to understanding the specificity of Polish rurality, where commodification of land, insufficient planning legislation, as well as social and economic transformation have their spatial consequences in the processes of dissolution in the countryside. The exhibition seeks new approaches towards the rural areas. It questions the definition of the architectural project, the practice and role of the architect in the existing context of the countryside. Therefore, for us to think of new rurality, we must challenge the existing regime, to seek ways of commoning – in effect to transform how a territory, a settlement, and a dwelling operate. Subversion of these three spatialities through an understanding of their historic ramification allows six European teams invited to participate in the project to present their proposals, to produce a new rurality. In the end, the countryside might yet again be considered as a paradise for us, but only when we overcome the trouble that it is currently facing.

Commissioner
Hanna Wróblewska

Curators
PROLOG +1
(Mirabela Jurczenko
Bartosz Kowal
Wojciech Mazan
Bartłomiej Poteralski
Rafał Śliwa
Robert Witczak)

Participants
Atelier Fanelsa
GUBAHÁMORI + Filip +
    László Demeter
KOSMOS Architects
Rural Office for Architecture
RZUT
Traumnovelle
Jan Domicz
Michał Sierakowski
Paweł Starzec
Wiktoria Wojciechowska
Patrycja Wojtas

Deputy Commissioner
Ewa Mielczarek

Organisation
Zachęta — National Gallery
of Art

With the Support of
Ministry of Culture and
    National Heritage of the
    Republic of Poland

Implosion of tower number 4 at Bairro do Aleixo, 2013.
© Nelson d'Aires

Retornados, boxes with the belongings of the families
returned from Angola after the revolution, 1975.
© Arquivo A Capital/IP

Presentation of Nova Aldeia da Luz to the population
by João Figueira, 1997. © Pedro Bandeira

Portugal

IN CONFLICT

City and Territory, as collective constructions, are the primary arena of conflict, understood as the action of opposing forces translated as dissension. This condition, implicit to a pluralistic democratic space, shapes architectural production. *In Conflict* responds directly to the question set by Hashim Sarkis – *How will we live together?* – by learning from processes that question the issue of dwelling in its physical and social dimensions, and where conflict plays a crucial role.

Public resilience and reflection transform these processes, which are still stirring, into valuable learning moments, to better understand architecture's transformative and political power. Recalling the portrait drawn of Portugal in the film *Non, ou a Vã Glória de Mandar* (*No, or the Vain Glory of Command*, 1990) by Manoel de Oliveira, *In Conflict* proposes a vision built upon a series of struggles that have yet to be overcome.

The Portuguese pavilion challenges the public to participate through two complementary moments: exhibition and debate. The exhibition, at Palazzo Giustinian Lolin in Venice, provides a narrative of Portuguese architecture through democracy, based on seven processes affected by material destruction, social relocation and popular participation. All of these were the subjects of broad media coverage, their struggles amplified by the press – taken here as a barometer of action and public involvement.

These processes are testimonies of a democracy that began with an impoverished Portugal, facing deep housing failures, which were aggravated by the demographic urgency of decolonisation. Today, more than forty years later, this reality remains fragile, marked by the persistence of informal neighbourhoods, by urban growth based on speculation in urban centres and by the abandonment of the interior of the country.

Based on each one of them, other projects with affinities to the problematic, scale or modes of action are called up for discussion. Thus, the debates – in nine events distributed between Venice, Lisbon, Porto and online – serve as an open forum around a prospective reading of the dimension of conflict.

Commissioner
Directorate-General for the Arts

Curators
depA Architects
Carlos Azevedo
João Crisóstomo
Luís Sobral

Participants
Alexandre Alves Costa
Alexandre Dias
Álvaro Siza
Ana Jara
Ana Luísa Rodrigues
Anna Puigjaner
Artéria
Atelier Conceição Silva
Ateliermob
Barbas Lopes Arquitectos
Bartlebooth - Antonio Giráldez Lopez & Pablo Ibáñez Ferrera
Bernardo Amaral
Bruno Silvestre
Carlos Castanheira
Carlos Machado e Moura
Cerejeira Fontes Architects
Charles Cossement
Colectivo Wharehouse
Eduardo Coimbra de Brito
Egas José Vieira
Fernanda Fragateiro
Fernando Seabra-Santos
Francisco da Conceição Silva
Francisco Pereira

Frederico Eça
Gennaro Giacalone
Gil Cardoso
Habitar Porto
Inês Beleza de Azevedo
João Archer de Carvalho
João Figueira
João Pernão
João Romão
João Siopa Alves
Jorge Carvalho
José Barra
José Gigante
José Lobo Almeida
José Miguel Rodrigues
José Neves
José Veloso
Laboratório de Habitação Básica (LAHB)
Luís Mendes
Luís Miguel Fareleira
Luís Spranger
Manuel Graça Dias + Egas José Vieira Arquitectos
Manuel Nunes de Almeida
Manuel Teles
Margarida Carvalho
Margarida Leão
Maria Trabulo
Maria Vale
merooficina
Miguel Cardina
Moisés Puente
Nuno Valentim
Patrícia Robalo
Paulo Moreira
Pedro Bandeira
Pedro Brígida
Rita Dourado
Rogério Ramos
Samuel de Brito Gonçalves
Sérgio Fernandez

Tiago Baptista
Vítor Figueiredo

....

Deputy Curator
Miguel Santos

Organisation
Ministry of Culture of Portugal
Directorate-General for the Arts

With the Support of
Fundação Millenium BCP
AICEP Portugal Global
Panoramah!
CIN
Trienal de Arquitectura
MIRA FORUM
Casa da Arquitectura
Público
Osvaldo Matos
Amorim
Expresso
Direção-Geral do Património Cultural
Sistema de Informação para o Património Arquitectónico
Diário de Noticias
Jornal de Noticias
RTP – Rádio e Televisão de Portugal
Espaço de Arquitetura

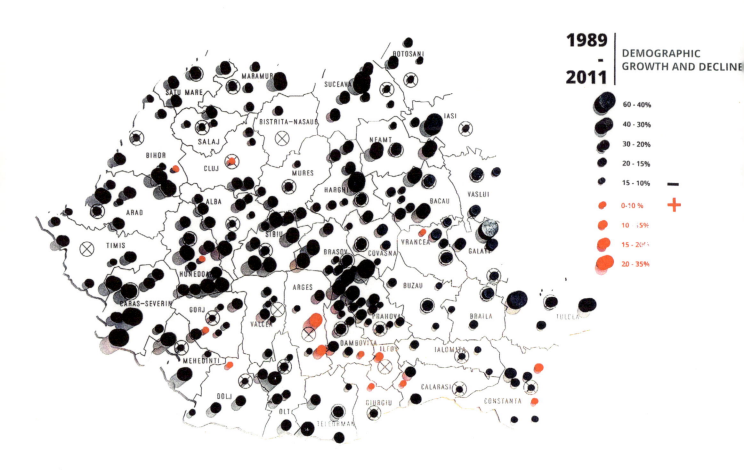

Demographic growth and decline of Romanian Cities, 1989-2011.
Map from the *Shrinking Cities in Romania* exhibition,
the National Museum of Contemporary Art, 2016.
Photo Tudor Constantinescu

Anina, Orașul Nou district, 2015. Digital, 50×33 cm.
Photo Tudor Constantinescu

Maxi (El Rumañol) on the beach Playa del Grao,
Castellón de la Plana, 2019.
Photo Cosmin Bumbuț / Teleleu.eu

Romania

FADING BORDERS

A dual phenomenon is currently taking place in Romania: 3.4 million people have left the country since it joined the European Union in 2007, while the percentage of immigrants coming to Romania has increased four times between 2005 and 2017, and now accounts for 2% of the population. The urban implications triggered by this process legitimise Romania to initiate a debate related to the role of architecture and urbanism in this new context.

Fading Borders is a curatorial project that engages with this topic by bringing together two complementary projects, *Away* and *Shrinking Cities in Romania*, each tackling the issue from a different viewpoint.

Away is the journalistic survey of Teleleu, documenting Romanian migrants trying to adjust to their new environment.

Having left behind their native universe, many of them are faced with inclusion issues within the local context (jobs, customs, landscapes). Still, new communities arise within the diaspora, bringing together migrants and local residents and creating new ways of life. This lively exchange of experiences challenges our view regarding what it means to live together.

Shrinking Cities in Romania is Ideilagram's in-depth research on the post-communist shrinkage of Romanian cities. Urban environments of different sizes and types (small touristic towns, large and small industrial towns, agricultural towns, old historic cities, harbours by the Danube) are now faced with various forms of decline: sociocultural, economic, physical, demographic. Rather than focusing on a pessimistic outlook, the study welcomes a constructive understanding of the phenomenon. Contrary to common wisdom, shrinkage is embraced as a vector for modernisation and innovation, re-use, alternative resources, artistic creation, and revaluation of interpersonal relationships.

As an outcome to the research presented at the Romanian pavilion at the Giardini, Mazzocchioo Journal is invited to the New Gallery of the Romanian Institute of Culture and Humanistic Research in Venice to add to the debate by gathering a series of contributions from acknowledged architects to answer to the question: How will migration influence architecture and the city?

Commissioner
Attila Kim

Curators
Ștefan Simion
Irina Meliță

Participants
Ideilagram
(Ilinca Păun
Constantinescu,
Tudor Constantinescu,
Iulia Păun,
Alexandru Păun,
Gabriela Belcineanu,
Laura Popa-Florea)
Teleleu
(Elena Stancu,
Cosmin Bumbuț)
Mazzocchioo Journal
(Ștefan Simion,
Irina Meliță,
Radu Tîrcă,
Cristian Bădescu,
Ștefania Hîrleață)

Architects
Radu Tîrcă
Cristian Bădescu
Ștefania Hîrleață

Communication Team
Dăescu Bortun
   Olteanu
Andrei Borțun
Maria Besnea
Simona Tatu

Graphic design
RIZI Design
Alina Rizescu
Bogdan Ștefănescu

Organisation
Ministry of Culture
   and National
   Identity of Romania
Ministry of Foreign
   Affairs of Romania
Romanian Cultural
   Institute
Architects Union
   of Romania

Gamer station videogame, Sanatorium 'Anthropocene Retreat'. © Mikhail Maximov

A glimpse into the gamer installation. © 2050+

Russia

OPEN!

The Russian pavilion needs urgent work. At the 17th International Architecture Exhibition, it will be open albeit under construction, both as an architectural structure and an institution.

Moscow, February 2021

These words, penned only a year ago, have a completely different meaning in the light of the current pandemic. How best to reflect on the main theme of this year's Biennale – *How will we live together?* – at a time of global crisis? We propose to rebuild the pavilion as an institution on a new and more solid basis by taking this project beyond the horizon of this edition of the Exhibition.

Aiming to investigate the public role of cultural institutions, on one hand the Russian pavilion was supposed to feature a new generation of architects, selected through an open call and invited to set up a temporary office within the pavilion itself. On the other, the building work was intended to serve as a catalyst for broader investigation into the politics of global events such as the Biennale, and an attempt to reimagine the layered system of rules, norms and relationships they are founded on.

In response to the outbreak of Covid-19 and the subsequent postponement of the 2020 Biennale, the Russian pavilion migrated entirely online, organically morphing into a digital platform called *Open?* (pavilionrus.com) and serving as an online journal for new contents and collaborations, while also building an archive of materials for Biennales to come. What was meant to be a physical space for encounter gradually became a virtual venue for a vast network of practitioners and thinkers.

In 2021, the Russian pavilion recalibrates its research focus by situating itself within the fluid, indeterminate space between the physical and digital realms. The project consists of three main components: the showcase of an almost empty pavilion, underlining the building's (architectural and institutional) renovation; a gamer station that reflects on the political potential of digital gaming environments; and a book featuring twenty-eight commissioned texts, examining alternative ways of thinking about and acting within (cultural) institutions.

The overarching goal is to explore how different realms – the physical, the digital and everything in between – can serve as testing ground for institution-making and other models of being together.

Commissioner
Teresa Iarocci Mavica

Curator
Ippolito Pestellini Laparelli

Participants
KASA (Kovaleva and Sato
    Architects)
Mikhail Maximov
Lion & Unicorn
Ilia Mazo
Yuliya Kozhemyako
Electric Red
Pavel Milyakov, aka Buttechno
Vladmir Rannev

Curatorial Team
Giacomo Ardesio
Erica Petrillo
Vladimir Nadein
Elizaveta Dorrer
Dasha Nasonova

Production
Altrofragile

Visual Identity
Lorenzo Mason Studio

Coordinator
Anastasia Karneeva

Fan Haimin, *Curve of life - Dance of angel*

Fu Yu Xiang,
The legendary Creature of the ShanhaiChing-singing with birds

Nie Jingzhu, *Medea*

Republic of San Marino

FRIENDSHIP PROJECT: SCULPTURE AND ARCHITECTURE OF ART

How will we live together? is the theme of the 2021 Architecture Biennale, a complex theme that naturally leads to many other questions. How we live in the future depends on the choices we make, in this case regarding the presence of architecture in the contemporary world.

The San Marino pavilion, in keeping with the plans of its curator Vincenzo Sanfo, aims to deal with the contribution that contemporary art makes to this new future. Art has often been eschewed by contemporary architects who, in the name of a vaguely defined modernity, refute in advance any attempt at adding 'decorations' to architecture. But then they will hide their architectural constructions behind trees and climbing plants, decorating anonymous parallelepipeds raised skywards, a hymn to an eco-trendy fad; or they will use daringly unbalanced forms to construct an attempt at deconstructing the concept of decoration itself.

The San Marino pavilion aims to reflect on these positions, and contrasts a series of Chinese sculptors and the work of two San Marino architects and a studio group made up of teachers and students from the University of San Marino in an attempt to pose questions or, if possible, provide answers to the need to recreate a sense of decoration in architecture capable of restoring personality to our cities, which are now all inexorably similar and indistinguishable from one another.

It is no accident that there is now an enormous world-wide resurgence of Street Art that is transforming the anonymous architecture of the city outskirts and, beyond that, of ever more visited places of art.

The pavilion also aims to use this contrast between Chinese artists and San Marino architects to celebrate the fiftieth anniversary of political-diplomatic relations between the People's Republic of China and the Republic of San Marino, which were inaugurated with the undersigning of an agreement establishing official relations between the two on 6 May, 1971, in Paris. The two countries, though very different in size, both have a thousand-year-old history and outstanding traditions, and are linked by a great friendship that has allowed them to stipulate cooperation agreements over the years in a wide variety of fields.

Commissioner
Paolo Rondelli

Curator
Vincenzo Sanfo

Participants
Fan Haimin
Fu Yuxiang
Fan Wei Min
Min Yiming
Nie Jing Zhu
Shen Jingdong
Wang Yi
Wu Wei
Zhang Hongmei
Zhang Zhaohong
Zhu Shangxi
Massimiliano Raggi
Enrico Muscioni
UNIRSM
Marco Nereo Rotelli

Co-Curator
Fan Weimin

Coordinator of the Commissioner
Riccardo Varini

Coordinator
Diffusione Italia International Group

Collaborators
Nadia Dionigio
Clara Mussolin
Giorgia Sanfo

With the Support of
Università degli Studi della Repubblica di San Marino
Beijing 2102 Art Center
Sculpture Magazine
Enrico Muscioni architect
Massiliano Raggi Architetto
Full Service Group
Matrix

Hotel Al Yamamah, Riyadh.
Courtesy the National Archive of Historical Photographs, King Fahad National Library

Aerial View of Dhahran from Corner of 16th and 'L' Streets, Building Under Construction is the Theater, Dhahran,
September 14, 1949. Photo R.E. Bright. Courtesy Saudi Aramco

Saudi Arabia

ACCOMMODATIONS

The growing shadow of an endlessly replicating microscopic entity haunts us. Over the last year, the spread of a virus has made the world intimately familiar with a concept medieval in origin and exceptional in its use: quarantine, a long-established strategy for mitigating the threat of contagion through separation. Viruses have historically been identified as potent metaphors for the foreign, the other, the one from elsewhere. The virus is a *hospes*,

Commissioner
Architecture and Design
  Commission

Curators
Uzma Z. Rizvi
Murtaza Vali

Participants
Hessa AlBader
Hussam Dakkak
Basmah Kaki

a stranger, a guest, and our response to it reveals the limits of our protocols of care and ethics of hospitality, which are determined precisely by how the self negotiates the exhortations of the other, one whose unfamiliarity registers as a threat. The most common response, amplified and accelerated in emergencies like the pandemic, is imagined, enacted, and enforced through boundaries and enclosures, both literal and figurative. They range in scale from the individual and the collective to the governmental and the national, bisecting both body and space into zones of inclusion and exclusion.

Accommodations analyses a series of spatial and social configurations of encounter with the other in which the histories, protocols, and gestures of quarantine, hosting, and housing are intertwined. Our use of accommodation is intentionally wide-ranging, extending beyond its traditional architectural definition of 'living quarters'. It encompasses the temporary and permanent structures that emerge to manage the threat of contagion, expansions of medical and housing infrastructures necessitated and intensified by the pressures of large-scale events, both planned and unprecedented, such as pilgrimages and pandemics. It also indexes the potential for transformation catalysed by crisis, its capacity to make space, addressing some of the ways in which the built environment and urban fabric accommodate the conditions of emergency, how the meaning and use of such spaces shift, and how sociality is negotiated within them. At the exhibition's core lies the desire to better understand the relationship and tension between the acts of separation inherent in quarantine and the acts of accommodation required to continue living.

Map of the Bor Municipality

Bor – Industrial Area

Serbia

8TH KILOMETER

The theme of the Biennale Architettura *How will we live together?* is interpreted through the *life-work* relationship that generates forms of collectivity and is manifested as the relation between one city's production base and its urban structure. The specific subject of the research, that forms the main content of the exhibition in the pavilion of Serbia, is the town of Bor. Geographically positioned within a non-ferrous metal mining basin, this town was urbanistically and architecturally developed during the post-war industrialisation period, thus further upgrading its multicultural character previously developed through the town's core economic activity – mining.

In everyday language, the residents of Bor refer to the individual places of the town through a measure of their distance from the Bor open pit mine, which they take as a starting point – 'zero kilometre' or 'the end of the world'. The inhabitants' system of orientation is analogous to the methodology of planning and construction of the town itself by way of *seven city kilometres*.

In the example of the Bor Basin, developed mining production is unambiguously positioned as the sole factor of the town's existence. By placing this production into global capital flows, the town exhibits the absence of opportunities to improve its social and spatial plans. At the same time, due to the unsustainability of the previously proposed alternatives to its socio-economic development, Bor also represents an opportunity to redefine the *life–work* relationship and consequently its physical framework. Therefore, the exhibition and research investigate the future of this relationship through the theme of the '8th kilometre' (a qualitatively new layer of the town of Bor) that introduces *disruption* into the order of the existing seven urban zones – 'kilometres'.

Commissioner
Slobodan Jović

Scientific Committee
Ljiljana Miletić Abramović
Aleksandru Vuja
Tanja Damljanović Conley
Predrag Milutinović
Zorica Savičić
Branko Stanojević
Dejan Todorović

Participant
Moderni u Beogradu
(Iva Bekić
Petar Cigić
Dalia Dukanac
Stefan Đorđević
Irena Gajić
Mirjana Ješić
Hristina Stojanović
Snežana Zlatković)

Realisation
Museum of Applied Art,
    Belgrade

With the Support of
Ministry of Culture and Media,
    Republic of Serbia
Union of Architects of Serbia

Maxwell Food Centre, A Hawker Centre in Singapore, 2020

Singapore

TO GATHER
THE ARCHITECTURE
OF RELATIONSHIPS

Singapore is a progressive city–state that has advanced through long-term planning and various urban and architectural innovations. With an ever-evolving urban landscape, Singaporeans have to negotiate the changing dynamics of configuring and redefining relationships with their city, each other, and nature.

The title of the Singaporean pavilion at the 17th International Architecture Exhibition is *to gather*. This presentation gathers visitors around a table to examine collective, ground-up action in Singapore. Drawing upon Singaporean spatial typologies, the pavilion is informed by a quotidian feature of Singapore life – the environment of a hawker centre, which is a community dining room with a diverse and affordable range of cuisines.

Envisioned to be convivial, accessible, and inclusive, the projects exhibited represent the cross-sections of culture and society in Singapore. They demonstrate how various stakeholders (architects, designers, community initiatives, and non-profit organisations) serve as catalysts in forming relationships, improving the quality of the built environment, and forging new spatial contracts and paradigms in designed and spontaneous spaces. *to gather* examines the role of citizens and impassioned architects in sharing Singaporean stories of living together.

The projects are brought together by four themes, which frame, contextualise, and examine the different modes and scales of gathering past, present, and in the future.

to gather focuses on relationships within local communities. In *Communing Relationships*, we examine how we can preserve and tap into collective histories so as to inspire new modes of coming together in the present. Built structures afford us a sense of permanence, and the projects shown in *Framing Relationships* are physical iterations about bringing different modes of living and working together within a single space. The projects housed under *Uncovering Relationships* invite and instigate a new understanding of each other and our surroundings through an embodied and multisensorial approach. Moving into the speculative, projects in *Imagining Relationships* imagine our future, conjoined relationship with digital technology.

Commissioners
Yap Lay Bee, Urban Redevelopment Authority
Mark Wee, DesignSingapore Council

Curators
Puay-peng Ho
Thomas K. Kong
Simone Shu-Yeng Chung
Tomohisa Miyauchi
Sarah Mineko Ichioka

Participants
Atelier Hoko
DP Architects
Drama Box, ArtsWok Collaborative and Forest & Whale
Hyphen Architects + Brian Khoo + Mary Ann Ng
Lai Chee Kien
Lighting Planners Associates
Michael Budig and Oliver Heckmann, Singapore University of Technology and Design
Millennial Nomad Space
MKPL Architects
NUS-Tsinghua Design Research Initiative for Sharing Cities
Red Bean Architects
salad dressing
Studio DO: PULAU
Studio Lapis + Eugene Tan + Jerome Ng Xinhao
Surbana Jurong
WOHA

Commissioning Panel
Larry Ng
Erwin Viray
Seah Chee Huang
Yang Yeo

Organisation
National University of Singapore

With the Support of
Urban Redevelopment Authority, Teng Joo Chong, Jeffrey Ang and Lee Lynn Wei
DesignSingapore Council, Yeo Piah Choo and Juliet Lim
Singapore Institute of Architects
Singapore University of Technology and Design

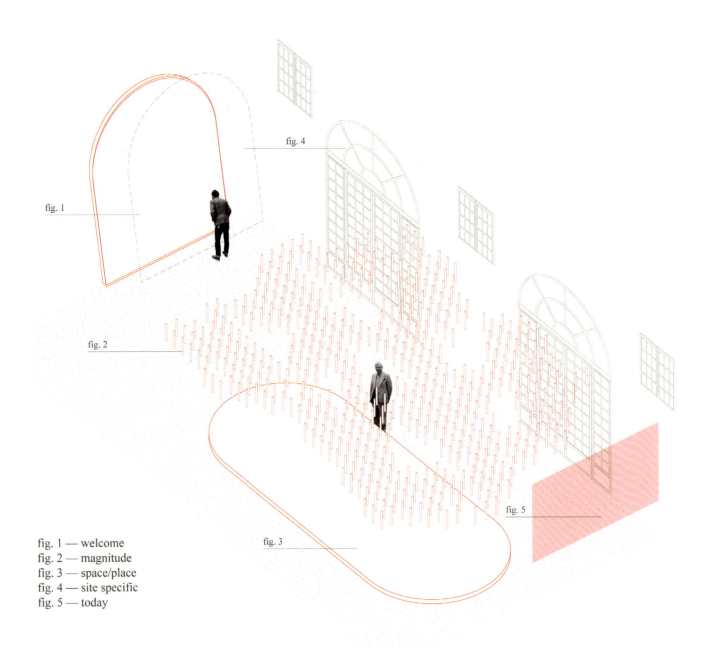

fig. 1 — welcome
fig. 2 — magnitude
fig. 3 — space/place
fig. 4 — site specific
fig. 5 — today

Axonometric drawing of the exhibition

Republic of Slovenia

THE COMMON IN COMMUNITY. SEVENTY YEARS OF COOPERATIVE CENTRES AS A SOCIAL INFRASTRUCTURE

The exhibition presents the ambitious project of building cooperative centres in Slovenia during the decade following the Second World War and traces their life stories to the present day. In seventy years of their history, cooperative centres have seen a change in the political and economic system, acquired new uses, and watched the lives of their local communities reflect the specific political situation of the time. Looking at the history of their inception and operation we begin to see how space can be secured for a community and the common within it, and how the authorities felt about associations of this kind through different periods.

The purpose of this Yugoslavian project was to transform social relations, decentralise the country, modernise the countryside, and kick-start the economy. A network of 523 cooperative centres was planned for the Republic of Slovenia, and 250 were constructed in only a few years. The authorities envisaged the cooperative centre project as a state-led plan with a well-structured organisation, planning, and communications scheme, with individual centres built by the local communities through voluntary contributions and shock work, which involved, in line with the principles of the new society, the equal participation of women and youth organisations. Cooperative centres performed a function that was cultural, administrative, economic, agricultural, and educational at the same time. They were meant to facilitate social and economic empowerment of the people and serve as a starting point for new urban development of settlements.

The majority of the cooperative centres have survived to this day, operating as publicly owned cultural and town centres. Some are in dire need of renovation, which would allow them to reassume their function, others are in full swing, having been renovated and maintained to serve the community as a form of indoor public spaces. A few have been demolished or privatised and wrested from their local communities.

The exhibition highlights the dimensions of the project in given geographical, organisational and social circumstances, both at the time of their emergence and today. Employing distinctive architectural elements, it shapes the character and functioning of indoor public space, whose role in the development and building of the community is underlined by the presentation of this project. Today, the subject of cooperative centres offers the chance to better understand the ways in which indoor public spaces can be set up as a social infrastructure that fosters free interaction and association, communication and empowerment.

Commissioner
Matevž Čelik Vidmar

Curators
Blaž Babnik Romaniuk
Martina Malešič
Rastko Pečar
Asta Vrečko

Assistant to the Commissioner
Nikola Pongrac

Pavilion Design
Obrat

Exhibition Design
Blaž Babnik Romaniuk
Anja Delbello
Nuša Jurkovič
Samo Kralj
Martina Malešič
Rastko Pečar
Aljaž Vesel
Asta Vrečko

Graphic Design
Anja Delbello
Aljaž Vesel

Architectural Models
Nuša Jurkovič
Samo Kralj

Video
Vid Hajnšek

Photography
Jana Jocif

Collaborator
Urška Cvikl

Coordinator in Venice
eiletz ortigas |
   architects

Production
MAO, Museum of Architecture and Design

With the Support of
Ministry of Culture of the Republic of Slovenia

Carmen Moreno Álvarez, *Celosía de memoria* (Memory latticework), 2017.
Laser cut black iron sheets, 3 × 1 m each, with a 4 mm thickness, along a 43 m line wall.
Photo Fernando Alda Calvo

Paisaje Transversal, *Joc de Barri #OlotMésB*, 2014.
Wooden CNC cut, wooden buildings and 3D printed
pieces for a participatory game model,
210 × 125 × 22,5 cm. Photo Paisaje Transversal

Sergio Sebastián Franco. Sebastián Arquitectos SLP, *Campanas*, 2018.
Polished stainless steel, aluminum, LED lights, 5 × 5m × 2,5m.
Photo Irene Ruiz Bazán

Spain

UNCERTAINTY

Certainty defines realities in which any kind of reflection or further study seems unnecessary. *Uncertainty* comes with the opportunity to generate processes that define those with a changing or unknown nature.

   Uncertainty, the project for the Spanish pavilion, presents a selection of several actions that hybridise and expand the competences of architecture to face new social demands, blurring imposed disciplinary and conceptual boundaries that have ended up becoming principles, thus creating open concepts from realities previously perceived as antagonistic.

   The exhibited works transform into a catalogue of architectural strategies necessary to face the new future of our coexistence and its social and environmental implications.

   The exhibition shows how social atomisation, resulting from the variability of responses to the uncertainty that we have experienced, does not eliminate the possibility of putting together a group or a community, and nor does it push us into individualism. Hence the central room of the pavilion becomes a volume made of hundreds of heterogeneous individuals floating in space who, regardless of their physical and conceptual distance, interact to build a single and recognisable body. A set of different architectures that, like the profession, is constantly transformed by its interaction with unexpected external forces, but without losing its ability to define a common path.

   Uncertainty urges us to open our certainties, focusing on the investigation of their limits and showing actions that allow different dimensions of reality to become open, dynamic, and adaptable processual elements. A future in which uncertainty, as a design strategy, has become the main tool to transform our processes and social models, breaking individualism in favour of coexistence.

   Is uncertainty our only certainty?

Commissioners
MITMA (Ministry of Transport, Mobility and Urban Agenda)
AECID (Spanish Agency for International Development Cooperation)
AC/E (Acción Cultural Española)

Curators
Domingo González
Sofía Piñero
Andrzej Gwizdala
Fernando Herrera

Participants
Carmen Moreno
Sebastián Arquitectos (Sergio Sebastián Franco)
Baum Arquitectura (Marta Barrera, Javier Caro, Miguel Gentil)
Joan Margarit
Recetas Urbanas (Santiago Cirugeda, Alice Attout)
Laura Muñoz
Ana Mombiedro
Sara San Gregorio
Alicia Gutiérrez
Cuac arquitectura + Sugar Platform (Tomás García, Javier Castellano, Julien Fajardo, Christophe Beauvez)
Paisaje Transversal (Jon Aguirre, Guillermo Acero, Jorge

Arévalo, Pilar Díaz, Iñaki Romero)
Milena Villalba
Santiago Hernández
Chenta Tsai Tseng
Sawu Studio (Aylín Vera, Pablo García)
CREUSe CARRASCO (Juan Creus, Covadonga Carrasco)
Contextos de arquitectura y urbanismo (Óscar Miguel Ares, Javier Palomero, Bárbara Arranz, Felipe M. Pou, Carmen Gimeno, Eduardo Rodríguez, Judit Sigüenza, Luis Matas, Sergio Alonso, Jesús J. Ruiz, Dorota Tokarska)
Miguel Arraiz
David Moreno
GARCÍA GERMÁN Arquitectos (Jacobo García-Germán, Raquel Díaz de la Campa, Miguel López, Marta Roldán)
Araceli Calero
Macarena Castillo
Rosa Gallardo
PEZ[estudio] (Maé Durant, Elisa de los Reyes García, Japi Contonente,

Blanca Villar, Viviana Peña)
Nomad Garden (Sergio Rodríguez, María Salas, Francisco José Pazos)
Antropoloops (Rubén Alonso, Esperanza Moreno)
Datrik Intelligence (David Solís, Juan Galán)
John Porral
Sergi Hernández
Hyperstudio (Diego Iglesias, Cristóbal Baños)
IAAC (Areti Markopoulou, Marco Ingrassia, Aurel Richard, Angelos Chronis, Raquel Villodrés, Starsk Lara, Diego Pajarito, Alexandre Dubor, Edouard Cabay, Kunaljit Chadha, Mathilde Marengo, Chiara Farinea, Mohamad El Atab, Federica Ciccone, Sotiria Sarri)
Animali Domestici (Alicia Lazzaroni, Antonio Bernacchi)
Natoural Group (Carlos Timoner, Juan Francisco Sánchez, Juan Antonio García, Pedro Milanés, Javier Torres)
Alejandro Cantera

María José Marcos
Fablab Alicante
Fablab Laboratorio de Artesanía Digital [L.A.D.]
Airlab (Carlos Bañón, Félix Raspall)
Quatre Caps (Bernat Ivars, Dídac Sendra, Juan Suay, Miguel Tomás)
Pareid (Hadin Charbel, Déborah López)
Alberto López de Lucas
Arquimaña (Iñaki Albistur, Raquel M. Ares)

....

Collaborators
Atxu Amann
Manuel Blanco
Belén Butragueño
Manuel Feo
Marta García
Juan Antonio González
Jorge Gorostiza
Mario Hidrobo
Francisco Leiva
Grace Morales
Mª Isabel Navarro
N'Undo
Juan Manuel Palerm
Gonzalo Pardo
Sergio Pardo
David Reyes
Ángela Ruiz
Constanze Sixt
Pedro Torrijos
Julia Zasada
Melián Estudio
Banda Bisagra
Lavernia & Cienfuegos

Mobile studio in Tägermoos.
© Swiss Pavilion's team of the Biennale Architettura 2021

Work on models in situ, Thal (CH)
© Swiss Pavilion's team of the Biennale Architettura 2021

Model workshop, Geneva (CH)
© Swiss Pavilion's team of the Biennale Architettura 2021

Switzerland

ORÆ – EXPERIENCES ON THE BORDER

The project starts with a preliminary hypothesis: if globalised metropolises have been the favourite playground of the twentieth century, the borders are now the laboratory of the political, social, and economic phenomena of the twenty-first century. Go slow for cross-border workers, hot spots for migrants, refugee camps, checkpoints, tax havens, duty-free shopping malls, casinos, brothels, principalities: at the limits of nation–states, an incredible assemblage of the residues of contemporary spaces is made possible by the border mechanism.

We never say 'I'm from the border'. We feel ourselves an inhabitant of a city, or of the countryside, but we are never from the border. This territory has no collective narrative. Inhabitants on the border, left to their own devices, have been thrust into the contemporary world in its most violent form of oppression. To date, the territory of the border lacks a political project.

To carry out this project, we asked border inhabitants to describe, imagine, and make models of their living space. People who experienced the borders of Switzerland, France, Germany, Austria, Italy, and Lichtenstein, as well as Iraq, Iran, Afghanistan, and Eritrea took part in this project, and a collective intelligence – a *res publica* – took form.

We chose the word *oræ* as the name for this project which is Latin for borders. It designates the boundary of something and, figuratively speaking, its 'beginning'. *oræ* is the project of a territory; its place is the borders, its actors those living within, its political and poetic programme inhabiting the contemporary world, starting from its margins.

Both at the Swiss border and in Venice, we propose different experiences of *oræ*: a sensory installation based on models and videos, a relational map, a guide as an invitation to a *dérive* inside this new geography and a mobile *forum*, as a place for political experimentation.

Commissioner
Swiss Arts Council
Pro Helvetia
(Madeleine Schuppli,
Sandi Paucic, Rachele
Giudici Legittimo)

**Curators and
Participants**
Fabrice Aragno
Mounir Ayoub
Vanessa Lacaille
Pierre Szczepski

**Collaborators
to the Curators
and Participants**
Noémie Allenbach
Benoit Beurret
Jürg Bührer
Annabelle Voisin

Project Assistants
Swiss Arts Council
Pro Helvetia
Martina Lughi
Anita Magni
Jacqueline Wolf

Pavilion Manager
Tommaso Rava

Architect on site
Alvise Draghi

Collaborators
Swiss Arts Council
Pro Helvetia
Chantal Hirschi
Lisa Stadler
Pierre-Yves Walder
Pickles PR
Caroline Widmer
Joseph Lamb

With the Support of
Canton of Geneva
City of Geneva
Bern University of

Applied Sciences
Ikea Foundation
Switzerland
Loterie Romande
Swisstopo, Federal
Office of
Topography

Support Publication
BSA-FAS, Fédération
des Architectes
Suisses
Fondation Jan
Michalski

**Support Mobile
Forum**
Herzog Bau und
Holzbau
Blatter
Holzbau Schweiz
Fankhauser
Fahrzeugbau
Blumer Lehmann
OLWO
Schilliger Holz
SFS unimarket
Bauholz Wenger
n'H Neue Holzbau
Serge Ferrari
HP Gasser
Media Partner
espazium

Special thanks to
All the inhabitants of
the border who we
met during the tour
and who contributed
substantially to the
project

Websites
www.biennials.ch
www.prohelvetia.ch

Boonserm Premthada, *Elephant House*, 2019. Photograph, 30×34.51 cm.
© Boonserm Premthada

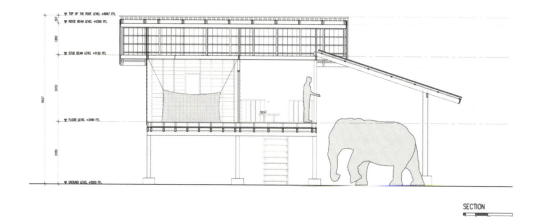

Boonserm Premthada, *Human Scale and Elephant Scale*, 2020.
Digital drawing, 42×29.7 cm © Boonserm Premthada

Thailand

ELEPHANT

Commissioners
Office of Contemporary Art
and Culture, Ministry
of Culture
The Association of Siamese
Architects under Royal
Patronage

Curator
Apiradee Kasemsook

Participant
Boonserm Premthada

Assistants to the Curator
Sompoom Tangchupong
Nawanwaj Yudhanahas
Salila Trakulvech

Photographer
Spaceshif Studio

Filmaker
Merage Motion

Technical Support
Jaruj Thammasoontorn

With the Support of
Andrea Marcon - Royal Thai
Honorary Consulate,
Venice

Thai Cultural Promotion Fund
Lighting and Equipment
Public Company (L&E)
SCG Cement - Building
Materials

The Thai pavilion examines how our architecture may embrace the other through an exemplary case between humans and elephants. Despite the distinct difference in scales and individuality, the way of life of the ethnic Kuy and elephants are inextricably linked. The past half century brought many changes that have altered how the ethnic Kuy make a living, their centuries-long tradition, and their relationship to other communities. What has remained, however, is the inseparable bond between the two species.

Albeit elementary, their buildings are embedded with much consideration for one another. Elephants are considered members of the household. A typical house is one where a generous section attached to it is dedicated to elephants. A man needs a shading structure, so there is also one for an elephant. There is a shrine related to their lives with elephants. A house will never cast its shadow onto the shadows of the shrine, and vice versa. And when one leaves another, there is a graveyard for the Kuy; and their companions rest in another graveyard nearby.

The Thai pavilion brings the house for the Kuy and the house for elephants from the tranquil village in north-eastern Thailand to Venice. These are not a replica but are reconstructed in a way that stresses the fact that one cannot thrive without the other. The structure of the smaller helps the larger to stand. And the roof of the larger shades and protects the smaller. The installation is accompanied by data on social organisation, a meticulous survey of the human–elephant houses and other shared facilities in the village, photographic accounts of how living together of the two species have impacted the environment beyond, and attempts of contemporary architecture to reinforce the relationship between the two.

Amidst conflicts and crises, our territory and another's may overlap more in the future. Another may be of the same kind or extend to other species. But in any case, the Kuy village may serve as a microcosm of how to live together – even for different scales and species. And their modest house will remind us that our future buildings shall also strive to embrace those different to us.

NEMESTUDIO, A Planetary Theater Play in the Diorama of Quarry,
Architecture as Measure installation (2020). Perspective, digital drawing.
Courtesy Neyran Turan. © NEMESTUDIO

NEMESTUDIO, Diorama of Maintenance, *Architecture as Measure* installation (2020).
Elevation perspective, digital drawing. Courtesy Neyran Turan. © NEMESTUDIO

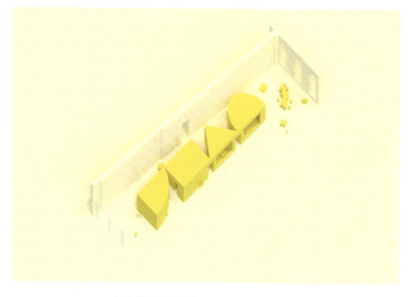

NEMESTUDIO, Dioramas in the Pavilion,
Architecture as Measure installation (2020). Axonometric digital drawing.
Courtesy Neyran Turan. © NEMESTUDIO

Turkey

ARCHITECTURE AS MEASURE

In light of the current political crisis around climate change, what can architecture contribute towards a new planetary imaginary of our contemporary environment beyond environmentalism and technological determinism? Rather than limiting the role of climate change for design as a problem to solve, can we speculate on architecture as a measure through which the environment might be imagined? *Architecture as Measure* positions climate change as a cultural and political idea that requires a renewed architectural environmental imagination. It provides an alternative perspective on the politics and nuances of the seemingly mundane aspects of architectural construction in Turkey via juxtaposing those aspects with their respective planetary counterparts such as geographies of material extraction, supply chains, maintenance and care. Working through storytelling, a physical installation and a publication, the driving prompt of the project is that architecture needs to see larger questions of planetary imagination and the everyday aspects of its own making as one and the very same category.

The exhibition installation comprises four diorama rooms. Each diorama focuses on one specific site of architecture – from resource extraction and material supply chains to construction and maintenance in Turkey – while allowing the visitors to walk inside the dioramas as if they are in the interior space of an architectural model. While the frontal two-dimensional view of the dioramas causes the visitors to experience the depicted life-sized event as a three-dimensional image, the documentary realism and exhaustive realistic detailing of the dioramas amplify this contemplative experience between the two dimensional and three dimensional. Moreover, because the visitors can enter and circulate in and out of the dioramas, the ideas of foreground and background are constantly flipped and negotiated.

In addition to the installation, the exhibition also extends to a website as its main publication platform and the curation of selected events in the pavilion. The website showcases the exhibition's research on the bureaucracy of architectural paperwork in Turkey combined with a series of essays and group conversations relevant to the themes of the exhibition.

In an era when humans are described as geological agents, architecture is a measure both to assess and to act upon the world. Through its focus on the relationship between the quotidian and the planetary, *Architecture as Measure* suggests another route for architecture's relation to the world, in which it is more of an agent than a mere respondent.

Commissioner
Istanbul Foundation for
 Culture and Arts (İKSV)

Curator
Neyran Turan

Assistant Curators
Betsy Clifton
Ece Emanetoğlu
Samet Mor
Melis Uğurlu

**Exhibition design
and exhibited works**
NEMESTUDIO

Editorial assistant
Ian Erickson

Visual identity
PALEWORKS
Ozan Akkoyun
Yağmur Ruzgar

With the Support of
Republic of Turkey Ministry
 of Culture and Tourism
Republic of Turkey Ministry
 of Foreign Affairs

Schüco Turkey
VitrA

Farah Al Qasimi, *Sabkha, Al Ruwais*, 2020.
Courtesy National Pavilion UAE – La Biennale di Venezia

United Arab Emirates

WETLAND

As the world came to a halt during the Covid-19 pandemic, local resources and production mechanisms became a necessary replacement for decades of industrial excess, one aspect of which has been the standardisation of the use of concrete.

Prior to the pandemic, we started looking into the sabkhas, a sturdy ecosystem of natural salt flats nascent to the United Arab Emirates, that inspired us to explore ways to produce a renewable resource for construction, one that can replace Portland cement. This is vital for our ability to live in this world. Cement production accounts for 8% of global carbon dioxide emissions, while its derivative, concrete, is the most widely used man-made material in existence, making it a significant threat to the habitability of our planet (BBC News, 2018).

We have always known that we can build with salt – the beautiful town of Siwa, Egypt, is a living example. However, extracting salt from the ground is not environmentally sustainable. The salt crystallisation process within the Sabkha offers a compelling model that we and a group of scientists at New York University Abu Dhabi, the University of Tokyo, and the American University of Sharjah have been diligently pursuing, aided by the fact that the UAE is the third largest seawater desalinator in the world (MIT, 2017).

The desalination process creates abundant amounts of salt brine with which we can reproduce crystallisation outside the Sabkha ecosystem. By using this by-product, we protect the environment from the accumulation of manufactured salt and, more importantly, we can create a viable alternative to Portland cement.

A synthetic structure made possible by our ongoing collaboration is presented at the UAE pavilion. Alongside it, you can examine natural Sabkha specimens, extracted from a landscape now dominated by jutting power lines and their ominous humming.

Without sustainable construction practices, we will further alienate ourselves from the world around us. Today we aim to usher in a new era of building with nature and not against it. We can do this by learning from the unconscious wisdom of the natural world and putting our inquiring minds to the task of harnessing renewable materials.

—WAEL AL AWAR AND KENICHI TERAMOTO

Commissioner
Salama bint Hamdan
   Al Nahyan Foundation

Curators
Wael Al Awar
Kenichi Teramoto

Exhibition Design
waiwai, Dubai

Photography
Farah Al Qasimi

Collaborators
New York University,
   Abu Dhabi
University of Tokyo
American University
   of Sharjah

Graphic Design
Sarah Chehab
waiwai, Dubai

With the Support of
UAE Ministry of Culture
   and Youth

Omaha Reservation, Nebraska, 1877.
Photo William H. Jackson

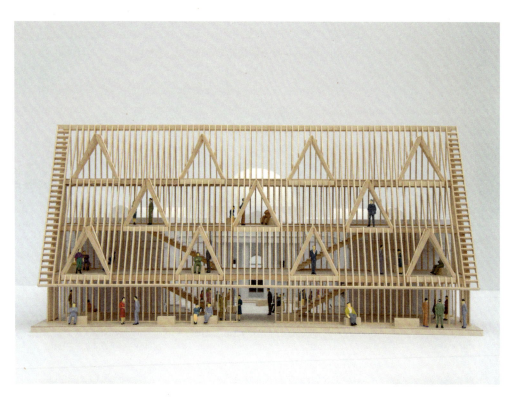

American Framing installation, US Pavilion.
Model photo Paul Andersen

United States of America

AMERICAN FRAMING

Commissioner
Paul Preissner

Curators
Paul Andersen
Paul Preissner

Participants
Ania Jaworska
Norman/Kelley
Daniel Shea
Chris Strong
The University of Illinois
    at Chicago School of
    Architecture

FDR lived in a wood framed house, Beyoncé lives in a wood framed house, and you can live in a wood framed house, too. Since its invention, wood framing has always been wood framing and no amount of money can get you better 2x4s than the ones in the poorest neighbourhood in town. To paraphrase Andy Warhol, framing is the same and all framing is good.

Because wood framing flattens typological and class distinctions, it is emblematic of American ideology. It is also particularly American in its history, design culture, and use. Originating in the early 1800s in buildings like George Washington Snow's balloon framed warehouse, wood framing was a pragmatic solution to the need for a variety of buildings during westward expansion. The availability of the principle material, simplicity of construction, and an ability to be built by low or unskilled workers led to the proliferation of a construction system that has since dominated the American built landscape.

American Framing elevates the profile of one of the country's most potentially influential contributions to architecture, which, for a variety of reasons, is one of its most overlooked. The exhibition presents the subject of wood framing in a collection of works. A full-scale installation forms a new façade for the historic U.S. pavilion – a half-section of a wood framed house through which visitors enter the exhibition. This open-air structure encloses the courtyard, provides space for relaxation, and expresses the sublime and profound aesthetic power of a structural method that underlies most buildings in the United States.

The pavilion's interiors explore wood framing's history and culture. Commissioned photographs address the labour, industry, and materials of softwood construction. Scale models present important buildings, common forms, and the potential of exaggerating some of the system's typical parts and qualities. A pair of furniture projects revive historic pieces by making them out of common dimensional lumber.

The works tell a story of an American architectural project that is bored with tradition and accepting of a relaxed idea of craft in the pursuit of something new. *American Framing* completes Delano and Aldrich's 1930s U.S. pavilion building, which aspires to classical European architecture, with America's ubiquitous domestic project: a wood framed house. It makes the case that a profound and powerful future for design can be born of an anonymous past.

Uruguay

PRÓXIMAMENTE

Throughout history, tables have worked as storytelling devices, becoming a powerful communicational emblem, in which the public and the private, the domestic and the territorial can live together. Whereas in Uruguay we are building the *black table* –a memorial site in public space-, simultaneously, the *white table* travels to Venice, a generous architecture proposed as a screen-table, an available field to practice 'proximate' futures. This table invites to take a seat, be immerged in ten human conversations, and be part of them, in a moment when 'proximity' has fallen into a crisis. These conversations, debates, exchanges and coexistences are consequences of a research and work process, which involved in its performance the construction of a filming set in Uruguay, which centrality was given around the *white table* and, at the same time, around the work with more than sixty people invited from various disciplinary fields, ages and contexts.

The *black table* is result of a public competition and consists of a large black metallic piece built in a public space in Montevideo, a memorial site, a resource for rethinking the past and how it is brought up to the present, a visiting table from a former prison recreated and turned into an urban table. As a complement, the *white table* invites to build a place of dialogue and a space from which the future may be outlined. Around the *white table,* politicians got together and made promises to citizens, a housing cooperative planned its manifesto, activists called us for upcoming demonstrations, a fortune teller predicted the future, scholars predicted their own deaths, teenagers proposed new cities, two enemies fought for their visions and friends celebrated when the table eventually collapsed under its own weight.

Próximamente proposes, from its title and display, trying out a playful answer to the Biennale's question. In its original language, not only does it refer to spatial closeness, but also temporal, and it is the term used for announcing an event, a new building, or an upcoming film -it is 'proximately' and, at the same time, 'coming soon', working as a foretaste of the pavilion, like saying: 'what you are going to see is a set of imaginaries under construction, an exercise, a heterotopic future, an invitation to create a closer world'.

Commissioner
Silvana Bergson

Curators
Federico Lagomarsino
Federico Lapeyre
Lourdes Silva

Participants
Eduardo Álvarez Pedrosian
Rafael Álvarez
Mariana Amieva Collado
Andrea de Aurrecoechea
Adriana Barreiro
Adolfo Batista Saravia
Silvia Bellizzi
Magdalena Bessonart
Verónica Caracciolo
Eduardo Carozo
Cristian Curbelo Cuervo
Cooperativa Covipedro
María De Lima
Bruno Del Puerto
Daiana Di Candia
Pablo Durán
Valeria España
Cristian Espinoza
Sebastián Estévez
William Falcon
Dina Fernández Chavez
Fernando Foglino
Olivia Fonticelli Amieva
Fernando García Amen
Lydia Garrido
Alfredo Ghierra
Cecilia Giovanoni Pérez
Nicolás Guigou
Florencia Lindner
Elisa Llambías
Ana Laura López

Mae Wilma de Ogum Iyaonifa Ifameji Odugbemi
Alejandro Mazza
María Noel Míguez
Sandra Nedov
José Luis Olivera
Lucho Oreggioni
Andrés Palermo
Ignacio Pardo
Cecilia Pascual Valverde
Lucía Pérez Pereira
Marcela Pini
Marina Piñeyro Rodríguez
Plan Ceibal
Cristian Rodríguez
Ramiro Sánchiz
Manuel Sclavo
Sandra Sifuentes
Carmen Silva
Willy Silva
Cristina Tirado
Daiana Torres Vargas
Marcos Umpiérrez
Carlos Varela

....

Organisation
Luis Lacalle Pou, President of the Republic of Uruguay
Pablo da Silveira, Minister of Education and Culture
Ana Ribeiro, Sub secretary of Education and Culture
Pablo Landoni Couture, Mariana Wainstein (Ministry of Education and Culture)
Silvana Bergson, Cecilia Bertolini, Verónika Herszhorn,

Maximiliano Sánchez (National Institute of Visual Arts)

Administration
Irene Buquet

School Of Architecture, Design And Urbanism - University Of The Republic
Marcelo Danza
Carina Strata

Collaborators
Cecilia Matteo
Carpincho Contento
Mathías Chumino
Luciano Correa
Mar Colasso Soca
Juan Pablo Colasso Soca
Marcos Villalba
Ignacio Correa
Anna Larroca

With the Support of
Communication and Publications Office, School of Architecture, Design and Urbanism - University Of The Republic
Ministry Of Foreign Affairs
Embassy of Italy in Uruguay
National Institute for the Performing Arts / National Directorate for Cultural Affairs, Ministry of Education and Culture

Republic of Uzbekistan

MAHALLA: URBAN RURAL LIVING

Historically built around family ties and the daily life of the community, mahallas represent an ancient form of 'living together', many variations on which can be found in large parts of Asia. In Uzbekistan, where the tradition occurs mainly as a genuinely rural space embedded within an urban context, this indigenous cultural institution takes on a specific meaning.

The mahalla is not only an administrative, hence geographic, division of a town, but also the institution that acts as a mediator between the state and society. Weddings, funerals, conflict resolution in the neighbourhood and in the family, administrative activities, and community celebrations are organised by these units, which now encompass all neighbourhoods in Uzbek cities, from ancient structures to Soviet slab quarters. There are currently more than 10,000 mahallas in Uzbekistan, each with 150 to 2,000 inhabitants.

Depending on the local culture, traditions, seismic conditions, region, and climate, different types of mahallas have developed over the centuries. Aggregated in labyrinthine systems, the historical quarters convey a sense of proximity and intimacy while creating precise spaces of assembly that the community puts to intensive use. The vernacular two-storey buildings made of clay walls hide family courtyards where local essences are grown, handicraft is produced, and gatherings are organised, similar to a rural setting but within a highly urban context. Due to high economic pressure, changing habits, and their lack of modern infrastructure, many are at risk of disappearing, even though they remain popular among people seeking an urban–rural lifestyle.

At a time when the ecosystem of the anonymous megacity is literally reaching its limits, the need for alternatives is greater than ever. Can the social organisation of these neighbourhoods and their various architectural formations as low-rise/high-density structures offer urban society a sustainable and ecological model? The exhibition aims at a critical reading and a tentative exploration.

Commissioner
Art and Culture Development Foundation under the Ministry of Culture of the Republic of Uzbekistan

Curators
Emanuel Christ and Christoph Gantenbein / ETH Zurich

Organisation
Ministry of Culture of the Republic of Uzbekistan

In Collaboration with
The State Committee of the Republic of Uzbekistan for Tourism Development
Ministry of Foreign Affairs of the Republic of Uzbekistan
Embassy of the Republic of Uzbekistan in the Italian Republic

Organising Committee
Aziz Abdukhakimov, Deputy Prime Minister and Chairman of the State Committee for Tourism Development
Bekhzod Musaev, Deputy Prime

Minister for Social Development
Ozodbek Nazarbekov, Minister of Culture of the Republic of Uzbekistan
Gayane Umerova, Executive director of Art and Culture Development Foundation under the Ministry of Culture of the Republic of Uzbekistan

Research and Development
Victoria Easton, Stefano Zeni / ETH Zurich

Collaborators
Giulio Galasso, Natalia Voroshilova / ETH Zurich

Project Management
Madina Badalova
Alsu Akhmetzyanova
Dildora Yakubjanova
Jasur Asliev
Jamshid Alimkhanov
Art and Culture Development Foundation under the Ministry of Culture of the Republic of Uzbekistan

Research Support
The Union of Architects of the Republic Uzbekistan Tashkent Institute

of Architecture and Civil Engineering

Associate advisor
Saodat Ismailova / CCA Lab curator

Consultants to the Research
Abdumannop Ziyaev
Shukur Askarov

Graphic Design
Francesca Pellicciari / pupilla grafik

Students Collaboration
Risqiyev Muhiddin
Rinata Mansurova
Saida Turabekova
Juraeva Munis
Laziza Tulaganova
Anastasia Galimova
Valeriya Kim
Kumush Muxam-madkarimzoda / CCA Lab
Senga Grossmann, Elisaveta Kriman / ETH Zurich

With the Support of
Saida Mirziyoyeva, Deputy Chairman of the Board of Trustees of the Public Foundation for Support and Development of National Mass Media

AMDL CIRCLE and Michele De Lucchi, *World Station, Education,* 2020.
© Filippo Bolognese images

Padiglione Venezia

SAPERE COME USARE IL SAPERE

How will we live together? How will we live together well? By creating harmony between humanity and the environment we live in. An imminent future made of light, culture, beauty, harmony, and a spatial contract. The Biennale – a free space for experimentation, provocation, and thought – becomes a place of questions: what is a city? Why do we live together? Traversing spaces. Replanning them, because the bases of living together well are also rooted in the improvement of real conditions of wellbeing, autonomy, and fairness.

The first space is that of living together – a social and spatial contract. The second is the complexity of the changes we are currently experiencing. The third is architecture's ability to create order, harmony, and beauty to assuage frictions – architecture is therefore an accelerator of the local economy. The fourth space is the vision of the possibilities of suggestions. The suggestions of Michele De Lucchi, who interprets space through experimentation, a reflexion on 'how we will live', a path made of visionary structures for a world in rapid change. We are currently living architecture to put people together, but this practice is no longer enough to maintain changes. We need to think of new places where 'being' is itself learning; stations from which to depart, destination Earth, meant as a place of knowledge and an asset that needs to be protected; Earth Stations, visionary images through which we are able to nourish the static imaginary of architecture.

These stations come into the world as monuments to humanity, its civilization, and they evolve through education, an investment in knowledge and human feelings that attract attention and inflect it in terms of an understanding of one's own Ego, of others, and of the sense of relations between human beings. Places of vision and, at the same time, of everyday reality. Because now it is not enough to know – we need to know how to use knowledge. And where to look for it.

New stations, yet other places of sociality and culture in the broadest sense of the word. Imagining polyvalent centres where you can tap into culture, education, information, imagination, creativity, study, leisure time, socialisation, and social cohesion.

Commissioner
Maurizio Carlin

Curator
Giovanna Zabotti

Participants
Michele De Lucchi, AMDL CIRCLE

Emilio Casalini

Scientific and Operative Committee
Elisabetta Barisoni
Massimo Monico
Silvia Moretti
Alessandro Pedron
Nicola Picco
Marina and Susanna Sent

Organisation
Fondaco Italia

Istitutional Partners
Fondazione Musei Civici, Venezia
Fondazione dell'Ordine degli Architetti PPC, Venezia
Fondazione Teatro La Fenice di Venezia
Ordine degli Architetti PPC, Venezia
Ve.La – Gruppo AVM

Partnership
Banca IFIS
Lunardelli EST.1967
San Marco Group - Novacolor

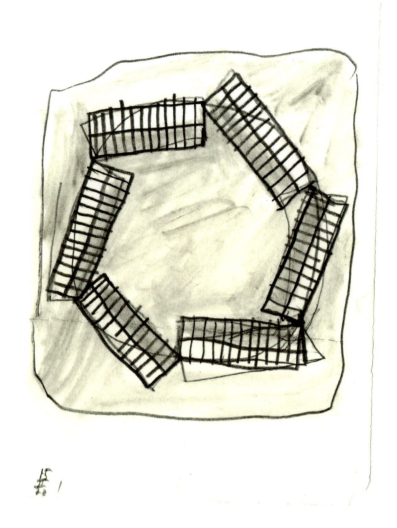

Michele De Lucchi, Studies for *Education Stations*, 2020

Michele De Lucchi, *Sapere come usare il sapere*, Venice Pavilion. Pencil on paper

Special Project Pavilion of Applied Arts

Three British Mosques

LA BIENNALE DI VENEZIA
WITH THE VICTORIA
AND ALBERT MUSEUM,
LONDON

The first mosque in Britain was created in 1889 by adapting a terraced house in the city of Liverpool. It was established by a community of English Muslim converts, who built a prayer hall in the rear garden and refitted the interior in a style that fused traditional Moroccan and Victorian decoration. Over the next 130 years, through world wars and following decolonisation and commonwealth migration, Muslim communities settled across Britain. Today there are approximately 3.4 million Muslims and 1,800 mosques across the country. The British Muslim population is said to be the most diverse in the world, with every ethnicity, language and denomination represented.

Mosques in Britain are grass-roots, crowd-sourced, community projects. There is no overarching religious authority that directs or funds mosque building; religious congregations are independent and self-organised, and anyone can start a mosque, anywhere. The history of the British Mosque is one of re-use, adaption and a layering of cultural identities.

Most mosques in Britain have been created through the repurposing of existing buildings, which range from houses, shops, cinemas, pubs and other former places of worship. As communities grow and their needs change the mosque is continuously reimagined. In a number of cases these adapted buildings, after serial extensions and modifications, are eventually demolished and replaced with a new-build that better serves the size and aspirations of the community. The purpose-built British mosque, therefore, has a pre-history of some 20 or 30 years of organic and incremental growth, leading up to its appearance.

Designed and in many cases built by its users, the mosque has generated an entirely new architecture for Britain. It is an architecture where the existing built fabric as-found by migrant Muslim communities has been reshaped to meet their religious needs. These needs are both functional and symbolic, to provide a place for worship as well as a vehicle through which Muslim identities, uprooted from places of origin, can be reconstructed in new ways.

The exhibition is about the way in which diasporic Muslim communities adapt and reimagine the built environment. In the making of this Muslim space a new aesthetic is grafted onto the existing city layer by layer. Part of this process is the reinterpretation of traditional Islamic art and architecture. Domes and pitched roofs are combined, minarets and gables are juxtaposed, arabesque patternwork and calligraphy adorn interiors. This is an architecture where the imagined is choreographed with what is found, and through this a new material culture is born.

As adapted mosques are in constant evolution, they remain ephemeral and undocumented. Without recognition and record, this significant period

Curators
Shahed Saleem
Christopher Turner
Ella Kilgallon

Participant
Shahed Saleem

Architectural Assistant
Leen Ajlan

Fabrication
Michael Short, Remshore
    Creations

Graphics
Boris Meister, V&A Design,
with thanks to Irfan Ahmed

Films
Julie Marsh

Project Management
Alex Willett
Catriona Macdonald

In Collaboration with
Brick Lane Jamme Masjid
Harrow Central Mosque &
    Masood Islamic Centre
Old Kent Road Mosque &
    Islamic Cultural Centre

With the Support of
Volkswagen Group and
donors to the Venice Biennale
Architecture Fund in memory
of Martin Roth, former
Director of the V&A

Harrow Mosque Mihrab and Minbar, 2010.
Digital photograph Shahed Saleem. © Shahed Saleem

in the religious architectural history of Britain will disappear without trace. This exhibition documents and illustrates the material culture of three mosques – the Brick Lane mosque, the Old Kent Road mosque, and the Harrow Central mosque – each representing one type of adaptation and stage in the evolutionary and aspirational journey of the British mosque.
— SHAHED SALEEM, CHRISTOPHER TURNER, ELLA KILGALLON

Brick Lane Mosque Exterior, 2016.
Digital photograph Shahed Saleem. © Shahed Saleem

Brick Lane Mosque Mihrab and Minbar, 2019.
Digital photograph Shahed Saleem. © Shahed Saleem

Old Kent Road Mosque Mihrab and Minbar, 2020.
Digital photograph Shahed Saleem. © Shahed Saleem

Collateral
Events

Barcelona redrawn by air pollution, 2020. © 300.000Km/s .
Data source: CALIOPE-Urban (BSC). NO_2 episode at 8:00pm,
11 November 2017

PM10 air pollution filters, clean and after 24 hours, Barcelona, 2019.
© Gunnar Knechtel

Air/Aria/Aire_Catalonia in Venice

INSTITUT RAMON LLULL

It is time to call for air design to be considered as part of the design of the city. The scientific community is not only alerting us to the global climate crisis caused by human action on the planet; it is also calling us to act in the public health crisis triggered by air pollution in cities. If the built environment is part of the problem, how can architecture be part of the solution? *Air/Aria/Aire* reflects on the role that architects can play in conceiving new urban cartographies with the contribution of scientists and the public sector, while also proposing new working methodologies that use big data about the city.

The proposal highlights the need for architects, architecture students, and other key actors within spatial design practices to redraw the city. All of them 'do' architecture when they design tools to empower citizens to collect open data about the city; they 'do' architecture when they analyse huge amounts of data about material and immaterial aspects of cities; and they 'do' architecture when they use this data to plan our cities.

Air/Aria/Aire is presented with an exhibition and a special issue of *Quaderns* magazine devoted to air quality in the city. The exhibition space hosts an installation that makes the air in the gallery present. It does so physically by showing the materiality of air, and in audiovisual form by mapping air in the city. The maps are created by the architects and urban planners Mar Santamaria and Pablo Martínez of the 300.000 Km/s studio, with data collection and other forms of collaboration from several agencies and organisations. Also presented in the space is a sound installation by singer Maria Arnal and producer Oriol Riverola aka John Talabot, who have composed and play for the occasion a protest *aria* dedicated to the air in which we live, invaded by pollution, which must be reclaimed as a common good to protect.
—OLGA SUBIRÓS

Curator
Olga Subirós

Participants
300.000 Km/s
Maria Arnal
John Talabot

Installation Concept
Olga Subirós

Exhibition Design
Olga Subirós Studio
with
Marc Sardà (sound design)

Graphic Design
Anna Subirós

Publication
Quaderns, Col·legi
d'arquitectes de Catalunya
(Architects' Association
of Catalonia)

Graphic Design, Publication
Bendita Gloria

Audiovisual Production
Fake Studio-Frankie
   de Leonardis

Collaborators
IDAEA-CSIC
ISGlobal
BSC-CALIOPE
Lobelia
Barcelona City Council
Government of Catalonia

With the Support of
Lamp

Website
www.air.llull.cat

Charlotte Perriand, Pierre Jeanneret, *Le Refuge Tonneau*, 1938.
Exhibition *Le monde nouveau de Charlotte Perriand,* Fondation Louis Vuitton, Paris.
© Adagp, Paris 2021. Photo credits: © Fondation Louis Vuitton / Marc Domage

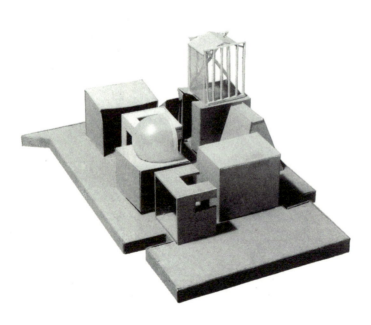

Frank Gehry, *Tract House*, 1982. Model, aerial view.
© Frank Gehry

Frank Gehry, *Tract House*, 1982. Model, plan view.
© Frank Gehry

'Charlotte Perriand and I'.

Converging designs by Frank Gehry and Charlotte Perriand

FONDATION LOUIS VUITTON

Curator
David Nam

Participants
Frank Gehry
Charlotte Perriand

Website
www.fondationlouisvuitton.fr

Over the past century, developments in technology have increased the frequency with which we have reimagined the home. Technological advancements, together with changing social values, enabled architects to invent new solutions for the way we live. From industrial to digital technologies, each era has brought forth promises of architecture's capacity to embody the times by embracing these innovations. Today, amidst an ecological crisis of our own making, we are attempting to house an unprecedented global population within boundaries that are in flux. The exhibition presents the work of Charlotte Perriand and Frank Gehry as both historical references and as viable solutions for the issues confronting us today. Two projects are exhibited for the first time: Perriand's Tritrianon project (1937) and Gehry's 'power pack' project (1969). In their respective times, Perriand and Gehry responded to the ideas of mobility, prefabrication, and efficiency and put forth ideas that redefined the home.

At the onset of the last century, Modernism took advantage of industrialisation to reframe housing as an industrial process. From 1934 to 1938, Perriand designed 'minimum dwellings' based on modular assemblies that could be mass produced and efficiently constructed. They were designed to have a minimal impact on their surroundings, while providing the essential amenities for dwelling. Perriand's understanding of ergonomics enabled her to design compact spaces that could accommodate the full range of human positions. Simple and elegant, they were to be built with standardised elements. Lightweight, they could be moved and reassembled.

The innovations of the space race of the 1960s enabled increasingly compact and efficient systems for life in space. In 1969, Gehry proposed a transportable self-sufficient dwelling unit. The project envisioned a separation of the 'mechanical, electrical, and waste disposal system' from the 'shelter'. With the potential to be run on batteries or a single power source, Gehry called the support structure a 'power pack'. The architect could design the shelter to suit any housing type, but the power pack could be a constant. Although the idea for the power pack remained an idea, Gehry's conceptual separation of the functions of the home enabled him to initiate his experiments in housing design.

In the context of today's ecological consciousness, the 'minimum dwellings' and power pack are precursors to current innovations in temporary shelters and independent energy collection and consumption. Their ambition to connect improbable utopian futures with concrete solutions is especially relevant to the real and urgent problems confronting architecture today.

Chan Ka Tat, Che Chi Hong, Ho Ting Fong, Lao Man Si, *Connectivities*, 2019

Connectivities: Living beyond the boundaries –

Macao and the Greater Bay Area

THE MACAO MUSEUM OF ART

Even now, the small city of Macao in immense China shows traces of the fusion of cultures in terms of its architecture and urban landscape, its peoples, ways of life, folklores, religions, gastronomies, and literatures. Currently, Macao is dealing with several challenges, including its integration into the Greater Bay Area of Guangdong-Hong Kong-Macao (GBA).

It is, therefore, in the connectivities among and between the domains mentioned above at various levels, in space and time, that architecture and urbanism can be seen as a pretext to reflect on the community and the individual's life, the community's collective memories, future demographics, shared spaces and architectural archetypes, and, most importantly, what we want for our daily lives.

Chan Ka Tat and Che Chi Hong explore the idea of connectivity that has developed ways of readapting architectures of various origins within the traditional architecture of southern China, which have been practised in this region and in Macao since ancient times, through long-standing archetypes that are to be reinterpreted in a contemporary manner. A difficult quest indeed!

Ho Ting Fong suggests a comprehensive tour around the urban development of Macao. He believes that the concentration, requalification, development of urban construction in the northern zone of the peninsula of Macao in conjunction with all the main infrastructures (both local and regional) integrated in the strategy of the GBA (be it built or currently under construction) will free and preserve the old city's urban fabric and its historic centre.

Lao Man Si proposes fragments of collective memories that are expressed in strips of floating cloth. The breeze draws gestures in the air with those strips of cloth that connect us to urban experiences, life, heritage, and different landscapes.

Connectivities take a hold of us, go into the future so that at a glance they can return to the past and persist in the present in the form of architecture, urbanism, exchanges of sensitivities, and individual and shared experiences. Will we live together? We most certainly will.

Curator
Carlos Marreiros

Participants
Chan Ka Tat
Che Chi Hong
Ho Ting Fong
Lao Man Si

Commissioner
Paolo De Grandis

Coordinator in Venice
Carlotta Scarpa, PDG
	Arte Communications

Website
www.mam.gov.mo

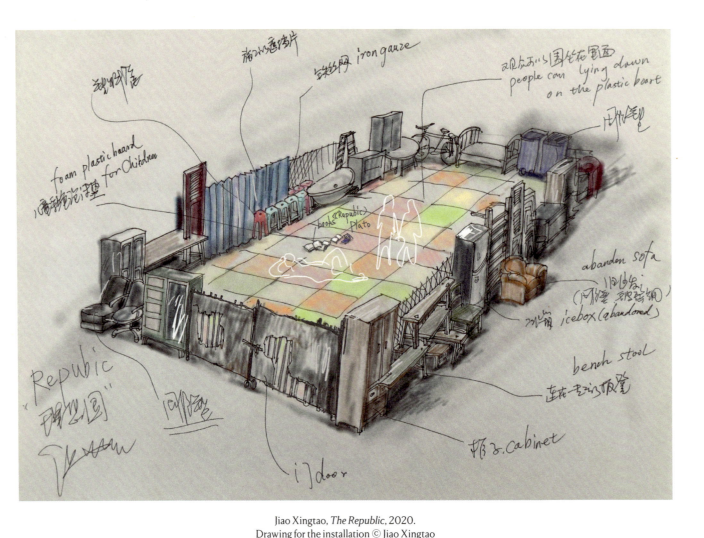

Jiao Xingtao, *The Republic*, 2020.
Drawing for the installation © Jiao Xingtao

Hakka Earthen Houses

on variation-Co-operative Living, Art and Migration Architecture in China

GALAXY GUOFENG ART

Immigration has become a cultural and political issue of common concern to people all over the world, and immigration policies in various countries are undergoing unprecedented changes. The conflicts, games, exchanges, and integration between ethnic traditions and migratory environments are the challenges and necessary prerequisites for the development of multiculturalism today. This cultural reality is full of contradictions and makes us all too aware that we must consider how one person and one family can live in peace with other people and other ethnic groups on the basis of respect for individual rights and family life.

Longnan County, Jiangxi Province, China is known as the Hometown of China's Round Houses, where various types of round houses have been retained. The large number, the various styles, and the well-preserved state of round houses all make this county one of the most interesting in China. As a physical carrier of local immigrants' living buildings, Hakka Round Houses formed a community under the turbulent times of the society of the past. They have integrated the three functions of family reproduction, ancestral family halls, and village castles, and this has created a distinctive architectural form and become one of the five major residential buildings featured in China.

Longnan Round House forms the basis of this exhibition, and is an attempt to search for the possibility of a positive interaction between people who have settled in different areas through the artist's sensitivity to the culture of immigration and through the creation of construction, the organisation of community, the reconstruction of space, and research and reflection on the history of suffering.

Images, videos, sculptures, installations, paintings, on-site performances, and architectural models are all used to demonstrate the changes and creative achievements of contemporary Chinese artists in terms of social awareness and creative concepts. Due to Covid-19, the issues of containment and closure, openness and communication related to human survival and safety are not only ideological, spiritual, and humanistic, but also regard the environment, space, and habitat conditions, and even architectural forms and patterns.

—WANG LIN

Curators
Wang Lin
Angelo Maggi

Participants
An Haifeng & Ying Tianqi
Fu Zhongwang
Gu Xiong
He Duoling & Shi Jindian
Jiao Xingtao
Li Chuan
Li Qiang
Li Xiangming
Ye Fang
Zhu Cheng

With the Support of
Tongmen Art Center;
Line Shi Yi (Shenzhen)
    Cultural Development

Website
www.chnguofeng.com

New podium for the village of Lianghekou, new pedestrian and cycle pathways.
Image Project Team

Grand Liang-Ting and *Silankarp* workshop,
two starting projects of the village renovation.
Image Project Team

Grand Liang-Ting and *Silankarp* workshop,
two starting projects of the village renovation.
Model Project Team

Lianghekou

Lianghekou, located at the Tujia ethnic area in the deep mountains of central China, served as a commercial node along the Salt Road which was a significant economic linkage in ancient China.

As a result of rapid urbanisation and population emigration, the once thriving village is suffering from economic decline and social exclusion. The renovation of the village of Lianghekou is part of a general masterplan for the entire Tujia valley, crossed by the ancient Salt Road. The general proposal aims to transform the traditional villages into a system of tourist services, accessible by visitors through collective transports or newly designed pedestrian and cycle pathways. The intervention on the Lianghekou village represents the pilot project for the entire valley system.

The project combines the renovation of the historical buildings with the insertion of new functions, preserving the identity-cultural heritage. In addition, the regeneration of the commercial street and of the system of common/collective spaces allows the reconstruction of the original relationship between the village and its surrounding landscape.

The architectural system of Lianghekou is typical of Tujia stilt houses, which are the remains of ancient *Gan-Lan* wooden tectonic culture widely distributed in the crescent-shape area in East Asia from Japan to Indonesia, including Southern China.

In the upcoming tourism development of the valley, Lianghekou Village is expected to resume its commercial and public function and to be revitalized as a gathering place for locals and tourists. The project makes full use of the variability, flexibility and adaptability of the *Gan-Lan* wooden houses. Through the transformation of the physical construction system, the ancient street is switched among different programs with topological deformations of public space from daily retailing to local market, and even festival celebration. The renovation starts from two misfit concrete buildings, which are designed to be replaced with a *Grand Liang-Ting* to serve as a public loggia for gathering, and a *Silankarp* workshop to inherit and present the traditional craftsmanship of the Tujia local brocade.

—ZHANG TONG, ALDO AYMONINO, ENRICO FONTANARI

Curators
Tong Zhang, School of Architecture, SEU, Nanjing
Aldo Aymonino, Università IUAV di Venezia
Enrico Fontanari, Università IUAV di Venezia

Participants
Aldo Aymonino
Giuseppe Caldarola
Dongzhu Chu
Enrico Fontanari
Cong Gong
Haiqing Li
Baofeng Li
Lin Qin
Aihua Shao
Shikuang Tang
Yuanwen Yao
Chuan Wang
Tong Wang
Tong Zhang

Collaborators
Students from Southeast University, Nanjing, People's Republic of China:
Han Xu
Mingming Sui
Yumeng Ma
Siyu Chen
Yunxuan Chen
Jie Shen
Hongyan Yan
Shizhao Ge
Shuang Xu
Rong Wang
Xinran Li

Students from Università IUAV di Venezia:
Giovanna Bordin
Ilaria Bottino

Davide Bruneri
Davide Burro
Alberto Canton
Elisa Cielo
Marco D'Altoè
Anna Marsella
Thomas Ortolan
Giacomo Rettore
Ilaria Rosolen
Alessandro Sparapan
Allegra Zen

Students from Huazhong University of Technology, Wuhan, People's Republic of China:
Ruifang Zhang
Shiwei Zhang
Rui Zhao
Yuanyuan Jiao
Zhuo Zhou
Xuewei Kang
Ren He;
Di Wei
Xiao Lyu
Zhiyu Yang
Xinqi Wang
Xiao Yang
Xing L
Shixuan He
Ning Wang
Wenyu Liu
Peize Wang
Changxi Wang
Xinyi Peng
Shuying Tian
Ruiqi Yang
Yazhe Liu

Students from Chongqing University, Chongqing, People's Republic of China:
Mingrui Gu
Chen Li

Jinjing Huang
Shuang Wu
Rui Yang
Lianjie Dai
JiaLi Pang
Danjie Shen
Yuhan Wang
Huimin Li
Bowen Tan
Yuwei Zeng
Guoli Luo
Shizhu Guo
Yihang Huang

With the Support of
The Municipality of Xuan'en County, Hubei
Enshi Tujia & Miao Autonomous Prefecture, Hubei
Southeast University, Nanjing
Università IUAV di Venezia
Huazhong University of Technology, Wuhan
Chongqing University, Chongqing
Thoth Hub, Shenzhen
Future City and Digital Architecture Association, Shenzhen

Website
www.emgdotart.org

LAAS, Augmented Common Spaces. © LAAS

Mutualities

INTERDISCIPLINARY
FORUM
NEUROURBANISM

We are in the midst of concurrent transformations, not unlike the generation who lived through the Industrial Revolution two hundred years ago. Significant changes that impact our lives can be found in the transitions from personalised control over devices to automation through machines, from a three-stage life trajectory to multi-stage lives, and from linear to circular economies. We will experience profound developments in how we work and educate ourselves, when and with whom we decide to settle down and have children, and who and how we meet in common spaces.

Mutualities highlights the interactions between people, common spaces, nature, and digital technology. The exhibition shows scenes of human activities in common spaces, which are central for people in their experience when common spaces become smarter, more autonomous, and self-learning. All scenes represent spaces that do not yet exist, for a time to come.

The mediation of architecture, spatial experience, and social challenges – such as cohesion and mental well-being – has been central to theoretical developments in neuroscientific research. Neurourbanism builds on this research to envision the 'city as it might be'. The exhibition turns into a performative situation where visitors interact with the digital world and become part of it.

This exhibition virtually expands the gallery into an immersive environment to experience alternative futures. The visitor's gestures can become signals that turn the exhibition into a resonating body. This space is always both – open and closed, private and public, narrow and wide, slow and fast, permanent and temporary – as are mutualities.

This experimental space captures visitors' behaviour and brings data and analysis to bear on how the notion of publicness changes in an increasingly digitised world revealing new mutualities. It encourages a wider understanding of emerging human values and develops a transparent connection between the analogue and the digital, between the architect, the urbanist, the scientist, and the citizen – altogether all the stakeholders belonging to the discipline of urban ecology who are engaged in shaping of future cities, villages, and landscapes.

Curators
Sonja Berthold
Dietmar Leyk

Participant
LAAS – Life as a
    Service

Collaborators
Participating
Exhibitor
LAAS – Life as a
    Service:
Zuliandi Azli
Pol Foreman Campins
Chrissie Muhr
Sonal Takar
Adrienne Wolff

Collaborators
Organising
Institution
Interdisciplinary
    Forum
    Neurourbanism:
Mazda Adli
Ludwig Engel
Joerg Fingerhut

Collaborator
Exhibition Design
and Architectural
Scenes
SPACECOUNCIL

Collaborators
Graphic Design
Catalogue and
Signage
Studio Joost Grootens

Animation
Scenography
Bloomimages Berlin
    and Morean

Motion Graphics
and Sound Design
Astronaut

PR and
Communication
Send/Receive

Coordination in
Venice
VeniceArtFactory

With the Support of
NEXPLORE
IBM
Vitra

Website
www.neurourbanism.org
www.mutualities.org

Not Vital, *House to Watch the Sunset*, 2021.
Aluminum and steel, height 13 m.
Rendering by Not Vital Studio. Courtesy Not Vital

Not Vital. SCARCH

ABBAZIA DI SAN GIORGIO
MAGGIORE - BENEDICTI
CLAUSTRA ONLUS

Not Vital is a Swiss artist who has travelled and exhibited widely since the 1970s, living between the United States, Niger, Italy, Brazil, and China. Central to Vital's practice is an exploration of the spatial and sociocultural backdrop of his homes and workplaces. Collaborating with local craftspeople and sourcing regional production, he realises site-specific projects in remote areas that are often hard to reach.

Curator
Giorgia von Albertini

Participant
Not Vital

Abbazia di San Giorgio Maggiore
Abate Stefano Visintin o.s.b.

Benedicti Claustra Onlus
Direttore Carmelo Grasso

With the Support of
Galerie Thaddaeus Ropac
Pro Helvetia
Wilde Gallery

Website
www.abbaziasangiorgio.it

In 2009, Vital coined the term 'SCARCH', a conflation of the two words sculpture and architecture. The buildings Vital subsumes under his neologism are formalistic and exist primarily to fill one single – usually poetic and transcendental – purpose, such as the contemplation of the sunset or the night sky. Crucial to his built structures are not the comforts of home or the way in which we might live in them, but rather the way in which they enable us to look at the world.

The centrepiece of Vital's exhibition at the Abbey of San Giorgio is an iteration of *House to Watch the Sunset*. Vital first realised this project in Niger in 2005, where he also built *Makaranta* (2003), a Koranic school for the children of Agadez which is shaped like a pyramid and accommodates up to 500 children. Like *Makaranta, House to Watch the Sunset* was materialised in close collaboration with the local community and sourcing the reddish clay of Niger. The building is 13 meters high and has three storeys, each measuring 3×3 meters and each accessed via an outdoor staircase.

Shortly after finishing this modernist yet archaic structure in Niger, Vital declared that *House to Watch the Sunset* would become a global project: on each continent, a structure would be built for the sole purpose of contemplating the sunset. While the materials of the building would always be site-specific, the form and dimensions would be the same at each location.

Within the Basilica of San Giorgio, visitors encounter the fifth and final iteration of Vital's global project. Materialised in aluminium by specialised Italian craftspeople, the structure is slightly reflective and thus in dialogue with the Renaissance architecture of San Giorgio, a sixteenth-century Benedictine church designed by Palladio. In exchange with the monks of San Giorgio, the artist decided to orient the work towards east, in order for it to also facilitate the contemplation of the rising sun – the symbol of Christ – which the churches traditionally face. The work's orientation towards the east puts it in dialogue with the tabernacle, the liturgical and spiritual fulcrum of the architectural space, and thus also enables it to become a *House to Watch the Sunrise*.

Apart from *House to Watch the Sunset,* Vital's exhibition also includes six other works, all conceptualised in reaction to the Abbey of San Giorgio and the city of Venice. Ranging from painting to sculpture and installation art, these works testify to the artist's multifaceted practice.
—GIORGIA VON ALBERTINI

siu siu, *Lab of Primitive Senses by Divooe Zein Architects*, Taipei, 2014.
Photo Jetso Yu. Courtesy Divooe Zein Architects

Primitive Migration from/to Taiwan

NATIONAL TAIWAN MUSEUM OF FINE ARTS (NTMoFA)

In a world that values efficacy above all else, globalisation has caused myriad environmental problems through the overconsumption of resources. How will architecture deal with this multicultural, vernacular environment? What role will architecture play in facing the contradictions between a highly developed civilisation and Mother Nature? What draws people and architecture to keep coming back to Mother Nature?

In the age of information, architecture must respond to the needs of the environment, the senses, perception, and the experiences of modern humanity. This year, the 17th International Architecture Exhibition raises the vital question of *How will we live together?*, which itself encompasses the subtopics of *Ask, Working Together*, and *Influence Each Other*.

Taiwan, located at the point where the Eurasian Plate and the Philippine Sea Plate converge, is such a tiny island with enormous diversity and its densely populated urban sprawl is unbelievably close to nature. Regarding the complexity of its mountains, canyons, animal and plant species, history, and cultural diversity, Taiwan can no doubt stand its ground globally. There is a delicate line between development and protection. The selected works display a variation of environmental conditions and industrial backgrounds, yet each piece possesses its own unique perspective on one common ground – and that is, architecture plays the role of mediator between the environment and humanity.

During the process of *Primitive Migration*, we try to explore our native lands and beyond, excavating what has slowly been forgotten, be it nature, species, or culture. Through the creation of space for living and the process of building, we learn from those are around us; we apply ancient wisdom to our modern-day life, and create far-reaching influence through cross-field collaboration.

Supervisor
Ministry of Culture, Taiwan

Curators
Divooe Zein (Tseng Chih-Wei)
Wei-Lun (Frank) Huang

Participants
Divooe Zein Architects
siu siu – Lab of Primitive Senses

Execution
Divooe Zein Architects

Collaborators
Double Grass International
Mauricio Freyre (Filmmaker)
Hung Chang Lien Elf-19 (Graphic Design)
Äi Äi Illum Lab (Scent Design)

With the Support of
Ministry of Foreign Affairs, Taiwan
Construction and Planning Agency, Ministry of the Interior, Taiwan
Taipei Representative Office in Italy
División Cultural, Oficina Económica y Cultural de Taipei en España
Taiwan Fine Arts Foundation
Department of Architecture, Shih-Chien University

Website
www.ntmofa.gov.tw

Redistribution: Land, People & Environment.
Carpentry pavilion, 196 sq m (area), 3 m (height)

Redistribution: Land, People & Environment

THE HONG KONG INSTITUTE
OF ARCHITECTS BIENNALE
FOUNDATION AND
THE HONG KONG ARTS
DEVELOPMENT COUNCIL

We have selected *Redistribution: Land, People & Environment* as our theme. Exhibitors propose solutions on the redistribution of these three critical resources to enhance Hong Kong's liveability in order to embrace the challenges and opportunities of people-centric urbanism and respecting the environment, both built and natural. The process encourages collaboration among members from corporations/large establishments, young architects/entrepreneur designers/artists, and researchers/academics/NGOs, which intensifies the search about the meaning of living together. The exhibitors showcase their thoughts on how to utilise available resources and their potential redistribution within the Greater Bay Area to improve liveability, assist the ageing population, and promote global talent migration, which leads to diversity and an improvement in Hong Kong's competitiveness. We demonstrate how to make use of technology and take advantage of Hong Kong as a compact, high-density vertical city, and how to take the lead in sustainable development, reducing the city's carbon footprint, and lowering environmental impact. The venue is deliberately 'disorientated', with outdoor and indoor reversed. The contradictions of the two distorted spaces and the reality of the spaces impose a question of how the surrounding context can affect one's perception of reality, very much like a social construct of what constitutes acceptable behaviour would affect what happens within a society. Exhibits are put behind the opening for observation, the setting denies the freedom of unrestricted 360-degree viewing, and the framing poses the question of what constitutes an objective presentation and whether a correct interpretation of reality can be made from one single viewpoint. How does one understand reality when conflicts arise as one changes one's point of view? Does reality, like society, take multiple forms since it is what one mentally constructs it to be? If reality is understood differently by different individuals by willing it into being, can there be a collective point of view, and if there is one, how can the architect access and align with such a viewpoint and create generous space to enable people to live harmoniously together?
— DONALD CHOI

Curators
Donald Choi
Benny Lee
Paul Mui
Agnes Hung
Ka-sing Yu
Hoyin Lee

Participants
'On Earth' Art
 Project
Andrew Lee King
 Fun & Associates
 Architects
Aravia Design
Arielle Tse
ARUP
aTTempspace/Easy
 VR/arQstudio
Brian Lee
Cass Lam
Chinachem Group
Chinese University
 of Hong Kong
Chu Hai College of
 Higher Education
City University of
 Hong Kong
Co-Lab Five
 Architecture
Dept. of Architecture,
 HKU
Division of Landscape
 Architecture
 and Dept. of
 Sociology, HKU
Dilemma Studio
Division of
 Architectural
 Conservation
 Programmes,
 HKU
Environmental &
 Interior Design,
 School of Design,
 PolyU
FAB-A-MATTER
Gary Wai-keung
 Yeung
Graduate

Architecture &
 Urban Design,
 Pratt Institute
 + Division of
 Landscape
 Architecture,
 HKU
Hoi-wood Chang
HSBC
Joel Austin and Kwan
 Q Li
Ken Lee
Knock Knock Ideas
Kohn Pedersen Fox
 Associates
Lot Architects
Make (HK)
Marco Siu
Maureen Hung
MBARD
MIT HK Innovation
 Node
Negawatt
Nikolas Ettel
No-boundary Design
OPENUU
Oval Partnership
Paul Y. Engineering
 Group
Policy for
 Sustainability
 Lab, Centre for
 Civil Society and
 Governance,
 HKU
Rocco Design
 Architects
 Associates
Roger Wu
SCAD
SHADOW DESIGN
Simon Ho
Sky Yutaka
THEi
Terry Chan
HKDI
HKU SPACE
The Mills
The Wharf Group
Tina Lam

Tony Ip Green
 Architects
Tse Yat Chi
Tsun-ming Ho
Tszwai So
via architecture

Coordinator in
Venice
PDG Arte
Communications

Partner
The Hong Kong
Institute of Architects

With the Support of
Create Hong Kong
of the Government
of the Hong
Kong Special
Administrative
Region

Websites
www.hkia.net
www.hkadc.org.hk
2021.vbexhibitions.
hk

Al-Nouri Complex after rubble removal.
© UNESCO, Moamin Al-Obeidi

Drone view of Al-Nouri before clearance.
© UNESCO

Drone view of Al-Nouri.
© UNESCO, Moamin Al-Obeidi

Prayer Hall seen from Al-Hadba minaret, 2012.
© UNESCO, Petr Justa

Stabilisation of the remains of Al-Nouri Prayer Hall.
© UNESCO, Moamin Al-Obeidi

Revive the Spirit of Mosul

UNESCO

For thousands of years, the Iraqi city of Mosul was a commercial, intellectual, and cultural crossroads, its very name – *al mawsil* – embodying the idea of dialogue and diversity.

This diversity, which is so central to Mosul's identity, is woven into the fabric of the city itself. It is particularly visible in the city's built heritage – its shrines, churches, mosques, madrassas, and cemeteries.

When Mosul was occupied in July 2014, this fabric was ripped apart. Over 36 months, violent extremists destroyed around 80% of the urban landscape, including buildings such as Al-Nouri Mosque, Al-Hadba Minaret, and the churches of Al-Tahera and Al-Saa'a.

In February 2018, the Director General of UNESCO, Audrey Azoulay, launched *Reviving the Spirit of Mosul*, one of the organisation's largest operations in recent years. Central to this flagship initiative is the project *Reviving the Spirit of Mosul by rebuilding its historical landmarks*, funded by the United Arab Emirates. This $50-million project aims to restore, rehabilitate, and reconstruct the historic landmarks of Mosul, and help repair the city's cultural and urban fabric.

On 16 November, 2020, UNESCO launched an open international design competition to rebuild the Al-Nouri Mosque Complex, built more than 840 years ago. The competition will select a conceptual design for the reconstruction of Al-Nouri Mosque and its Prayer Hall as they were in 2017, and for the construction of additional buildings for educational, social, and cultural activities. The competition's format was chosen by the project's Steering Committee – composed of representatives of the Iraqi Government, UNESCO, and the UAE – to take into account the cultural significance of the site.

An international, independent jury of nine experts has now selected the top five entries in this competition. These are featured in this exhibition, one of the collateral events at the Venice Architecture Biennale, which also showcases UNESCO's approach to supporting the recovery of the Old City of Mosul.

To launch the exhibition, UNESCO is hosting a high-level panel on recovery and reconstruction in post-conflict, post-disaster, and transition contexts, with experts from the fields of architecture, heritage conservation, and culture among others.

Curator
Sara Noshadi

Participants
5 runner-ups of the architectural competition for the reconstruction and rehabilitation of the Al-Nouri Complex in Mosul

Collaborators
UNESCO Team in Iraq
Paolo Fontani
Maria Rita Acetoso
Nuria Roca-Ruiz

UNESCO Team at the Headquarters
Lazare Eloundou Assomo
Nada Al-Hassan
Alessandra Borchi
Karim Hendili

With the Support of
United Arab Emirates Ministry of Culture and Youth

Website
en.unesco.org

Outtake from a photo essay by Mathias Renner
produced for *Salon Suisse*, 2021

Salon Suisse 2021: Bodily Encounters

SWISS ARTS COUNCIL PRO HELVETIA

The *Salon Suisse* offers a series of lectures, talks, performances, and cultural events supplementing the exhibition at the Swiss Pavilion.

Bodily Encounters revolves around the fundamental relationships between body and architecture: when space is being experienced, the body serves as the most important system of orientation and measurement. Architecture protects the body, extends it, and condenses its memories. Furthermore, the built environment touches all our senses and influences our psyche. Finally, architecture itself constitutes a body and a living organism, especially with regard to the increasing interconnectedness of the physical and virtual world.

As the current pandemic continues to disrupt and challenge our ways of working and co-living on different scales, it is of paramount importance to renegotiate the substantial interdependencies between body and space. In view of formalised social control and an ongoing disassociation with the environment, we must come up with new spatial imaginations that encourage and stimulate human and cultural exchange.

Following the tradition of the *Salon* and its claim of reigniting a culture of stimulating debate and social encounter in an agreeable ambience, the manifold encounters between body and architecture are examined from different perspectives, concentrating on three topics. At the first *Salon* in September, the emphasis is on viewing built structures as animated independent organisms, the spatial gestures of which enter into a dialogue with the human being. The *Salon* in October focuses on how architecture creates standardised realities that define our coexistence. Within the third and last *Salon* in November, bodily alterations and optimisation measures, such as body hacking or anti-ageing procedures, are assessed and adapted for architectural discourse. As a result of its broad approach, *Salon Suisse* deals with a multitude of disciplines and themes, such as transhumanism, psychoanalysis, neurosciences, literature, interior design, disability studies, fluid spaces, medical anthropology, mood-sensitive houses, and many more.

This is all geared towards not only those involved in the practice and teaching of architecture, but also, most importantly, everyday experts who wish to enrich the discipline of architecture with their knowledge – in short, anyone who wants to have new *bodily encounters* and experiences, and to explore the multifarious dimensions of the body and architecture.
— EVELYN STEINER

Curator
Evelyn Steiner

Participants
Mounir Ayoub
Andrea Bagnato
Oliver Bendel
Ana Dana Beroš
Jos Boys
Graeme Brooker
Dora Budor
Nicolas Delaroche
Ingrid Feigl
Andri Gerber
Jannik Giger
Deborah Howard
Jessica Huber
Lydia Kallipoliti
Florine Leoni
Tim Kammasch
Andrejs Krutojs
Vanessa Lacaille
Jelena Martinovic
Andrew Paice
Jessy Razafimandimby
Nathalie Rebholz
Joel Sanders
Davide-Christelle Sanvee
Mike Schaffner
Tiberio Scozzafava-Jaeger
David Spurr
Christof Stürchler
Irene Sunwoo
Georg Vrachliotis
Katharina Anna Wieser
Stanislas Zimmermann
and others

Assistant to the Curator
Viviane Ehrensberger

With the Support of
LAUFEN Bathrooms

Websites
www.prohelvetia.ch
www.biennials.ch

Svetlana Kana Radevic, Hotel Podgorica. Unknown photographer.
Archive of Pobjeda

Svetlana Kana Radevic, Bus station Podgorica, 1968.
Photograph from the personal archive of the author

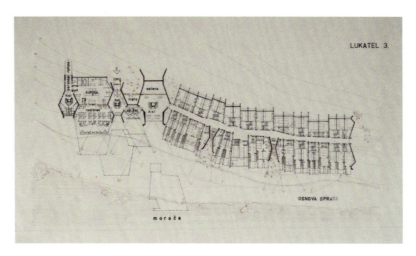

Svetlana Kana Radević, Architectural drawing, Hotel Podgorica.
Architect's archive

Skirting The Center:
Svetlana Kana Radević on the Periphery of Postwar Architecture

APSS INSTITUTE

Both in her built work and in the geopolitical circumstances of her professional life, Svetlana Kana Radević (1937–2000) posited the figure of the architect as a mediating force across societal registers: regionally, negotiating between a vernacular building tradition and the globalising tendencies of late modernism; nationally, designing celebrated civic spaces and social condensers that facilitated a progressive public sphere between the socialist state and its citizenry; and internationally, articulating a decentred, postcolonial axis by which the Montenegrin architect simultaneously and seamlessly worked between Philadelphia, Tokyo, and Podgorica. A protégée of both Louis Kahn and Kisho Kurokawa, and among the most prominent architects in socialist Yugoslavia, Radević designed anti-fascist memorials, hotels, and residential projects – celebrated for their deft synthesis of local materials and international tendencies, as well as a generosity of proportions and informal spaces for leisure and exchange – but remains almost completely unknown internationally. This exhibition shows original drawings, photographs, and correspondences from her personal archive, a trove of newly discovered materials that make it possible to contextualise and historicise an exceptional, overlooked figure whose oeuvre suggests possibilities for a renewed spatial contract based on an ethos of radical collectivity and local specificity.

Radević remains the only woman and, at 29, the youngest person to ever win the prestigious Borba Architecture Prize, socialist Yugoslavia's highest architectural honour, which she received in 1969.

Radević subverted hierarchies that privilege cosmopolitan centres over provincial peripheries by locating her personal practice in Montenegro. Yet her architecture was ultimately supranational, simultaneously digesting vernacular building traditions as well as her global study and work experience.

A handful of drawings from her archive were shown publicly for the first time as part of *Toward a Concrete Utopia: Architecture in Yugoslavia, 1948–1980* at the Museum of Modern Art, New York.

Curators
Dijana Vučinić
Anna Kats

Communication and Marketing
Katarina Milačić

Graphic Design and Photography
Luka Bošković

Production Assistant
Dea Đebrić

With the Support of
President of Montenegro
Capital City of Podgorica

Additional Support
Ministry of Culture of
    Montenegro
CEDIS
GLOSARIJ
Montenegro Metropolis Media
Hipotekarna Banka
BEMAX
Savana
UNIPROM-KAP
RTVCG
Univerzitet CG

Website
www.kotorapss.me

Bamboo Majlis, 2019. *Majlis* prototyping in Colombia.
Photo Jörg Gruber

Shepherd Family, Atlas Mountains, Morocco, 2019.
Photo Jörg Gruber for Caravane Foundation

The Majlis

CARAVANE EARTH FOUNDATION

'Your house is your larger body. It grows in the sun and sleeps in the stillness of the night; and it is not dreamless'.
Khalil Gibran

Curator
Thierry Morel

Participants
Simón Vélez
Stefana Simić
Todd Longstaffe-Gowan
Ahmed Chmiti
Omar Zaidani
Yihya Yihyawi
Hashima A'douri
Nina Mohammad-Galbert
Irini Gonou
Ira Sokolova
Studio DA
NMoQ (National Museum of Qatar)
Nationaal Museum van Wereldculturen
Claudio Cravero
Sheikh Faisal Bin Qassim Al Thani Museum
INBTAU
UNESCO
Johnny Cornwell
Science & Human Dimension Project

Abbazia di San Giorgio Maggiore
Abate Stefano Visintin o.s.b.

Benedicti Claustra Onlus
Direttore Carmelo Grasso

Website
www.caravane.earth

Caravane Earth Foundation, within the cultural activities of the Benedicti Claustra, the non-profit branch of the Abbazia di San Giorgio Maggiore, presents the *Majlis*. Designed by natural material pioneers Simón Vélez and Stefana Simić in Colombia, in collaboration with Ahmed Chmiti and the Boujad Women's Weaving Collective in Morocco, the *Majlis* is situated in the garden of the Benedictine monastery with a new project created on purpose by landscape architect Todd Longstaffe-Gowan. Inspired by nomadic architecture, the *Majlis* is made from bamboo, the most renewable building material on earth, and shrouded in textiles handwoven in the Atlas Mountains of Morocco. In the *majlis*, ancient building traditions are complemented by the latest construction technologies, allowing age-old forms to flourish in a contemporary context.

In 2015, the *majlis* was added to UNESCO's Representative List of the Intangible Cultural Heritage of Humanity as a social and cultural space: '*Majlis* are "sitting places" where community members gather to discuss local events and issues, resolve problems, exchange news, receive guests, socialise, and be entertained'. In Venice, the *Majlis* is a space for storytelling, symposia, and exchange between East and West, all in an effort to reflect on the theme of the 17th International Architecture Exhibition, the question posed by Biennale curator Hashim Sarkis: *How will we live together?*

The *Majlis* installation and exhibition explore the careful sourcing of materials, ethical processes of production, and feature the expertise of contemporary craftspeople, while contextualising the *majlis* in history through artefacts and art works. The *Majlis* events programme brings to Venice international thinkers and experts from a wide variety of backgrounds, addressing the Biennale theme and the ultimate purpose of Caravane Earth Foundation's activity: the empowerment of local communities by reviving artisanship and vernacular architecture, and the revitalisation of local natural resources and ecosystems.

Coldefy, Tropicalia, 2023.
Image Octav Tiraziu © Coldefy

Coldefy, Tropicalia, 2023.
Image Octav Tiraziu © Coldefy

Tropicalia. Architecture, Materials, Innovative Systems

ZUECCA PROJECTS

Cities are fast growing and changing, the quality of air is increasingly impacted as we experience the effects of climate change. The balance between hardscape and softscape becomes difficult to manage. Facts and figures are becoming a new source of anxiety, as data continually enter our lives unwillingly. In anthropology, the *domus* was a unique and unprecedented phenomenon, consisting of an ensemble of tilled fields, seed and grain stores, people, and domestic animals, all co-evolving with effects no one could possibly have foreseen.

The exhibition *Tropicalia. Architecture, Materials, Innovative Systems*, situated in the phantasmatic city grid of Venice, questions the impact of manmade structures in our daily lives and opens a broader discussion on the impact and experience of the question 'Where does architecture stand today?'
—THOMAS COLDEFY

The theme *domus* is illustrated with emblematic research and documentation of the giant greenhouse Tropicalia that will be completed and delivered in 2023 in Rang-du-Fliers, northern France, designed by the architecture firm Coldefy. The exhibition presents the current state of the research on tropical fauna and flora – led by LabEx CEBA, a French laboratory working on Amazonian biodiversity – and its benefits to the ecosystem, the planet, and health. It also presents the architectural and engineering specificities of the greenhouse Tropicalia that will be the biggest in the world, as well as its unique sustainable air treatment engineering.

Illustrated by architectural models, drawings, sketches, and diverse working and presentation materials, the exhibition transmits an environmental and educational message: it shows how science can answer the question *How will we live together?*

It also makes the visitor discover the engineering and architectural prowess and uniqueness of the future giant greenhouse Tropicalia.

Curators
Thomas Coldefy
Alessandro Possati

Participant
Coldefy

Project Coordinator
Maria Caterina Denora

Exhibition Designer
Marianna Guarino

Communications and
Development Director
Elisabeth Girot

With the Support of
Autodesk
Lenovo
Tarkett
Novaxia
Hausbrandt Trieste 1892
LabEx CEBA – Centre
    d'Étude de la Biodiversité
    Amazonienne
Alliance française

Website
www.zueccaprojects.org

Collective artwork, *Without Land/ Pomerium*, 2020

Without Land / Pomerium

A.I.A.P. (ASSOCIAZIONE INTERNAZIONALE ARTI PLASTICHE)

In an ever more divided and disrupted society (liquid to some), already folded in on the individual, or at best on the ideological 'tribe', the *Without Land/Pomerium* project attempts to establish a place of refuge, a point of access or trespassing, in conclusion a *nonplace* in which one can find shelter and humanity in a united civilisation that accepts everyone in need, without distinction of social class or race, for the sake of the sacred community.

The project consists of an upside-down boat, supported on top by its own oars. The boat therefore becomes a shelter from bad weather and a place to meditate, for any kind of castaway. The fact that it is only a hull-shaped roof – just like those that can currently be found in community architectures such as churches and civil buildings – denotes the memory of a common past that has been erected as if it were a monument, an eternal memento for the ages. To find the origins is to return to the original historic community that symbolises a unity akin to the entire human race, without any distinction.

Curator
Boris Brollo

Participants
Andrea Rossi Andrea
Emiliano Bazzanella
Stefania Basso
Giuliana Bellini
Bluer
Alda Boscaro
Svetlana Boyarkina
Clara Brasca
Paola Bradamante
Carmine Calvanese
Carmela Candido
Giulio Candussio
Giancarlo Caneva
Marcello Caporale
Domenico Castaldi
Gianpietro Cavedon
Auro e Celso Ceccobelli
Pino Chimenti
Milena Crupi
Bruno Donzelli
Carlo Fontana
Mirko Filipuzzi
Ferruccio Gard
Mauro Gentile
Giovanni Grigolini
Maria Luisa Liviero
Stella Lubuzhskaya
Roberto Lucato
Paolo Marazzi
Carla Galli Morandi
Melchiorre Napolitano
Lucia Paese
Biagio Pancino
Franz Pelizza
Mauro Peloso
Giuseppina Pioli
Claudia Raza
Carla Rigato
Pietro Ronzat
Giovanni Ronzoni
Alessio Serpetti
Lucio, Tiziano e Cesare Serafino
Simon Ostan Simone
Rosa Spina
Pier Toffoletti
Lucia Tomasi
Giovanni Toniatti Giacometti
Loris Andrea Vianello
Luciana Zabarella
Antonio Zucchiatti

....

Design
Boris Brollo

Scientific Committee
Francesco Tullio Altan
Andrea Rossi Andrea
Bruno Ceccobelli
Ferruccio Gard
Carlo Motta
Annamaria Poggioli
Ernesto Tatafiore
Lucia Tomasi

Project and Exhibition Setup
Antonio Candussio
Camilla Tomasi
Sonia Paolone

Communication
Sara Carnelos
Emidio Di Carlo
Ketra (Elena Pizzato)
Arianna Sartori
Roberto Vidali
Giovanna Barbero

Graphic Design
Sandro Corazza

Under the Auspices of
Regione del Veneto

Città Metropolitana di Venezia
Comune di Portogruaro
Comune di Spilimbergo

In Collaboration with
M.A.C.A. Museo Arte Contemporanea Acri, Cosenza
Circolo Culturale 'Spazio Arte', L'Aquila
Archivio Storico Tono Zancanaro', Padova

Gruppo Giovani Pittori Spilimberghesi Spilimbergo

Special Guests
Alberto Fol
Giulia Pes
Riccardo Pes

With the Support of
Nuovi Spazi Pubblicità
Artestruttura, servizi per l'arte Udine
Zanutta: una casa da vivere
Hotel Danieli, Venice

CA' ASI exhibition center.
© G. Fessy

Young European Architects

CA'ASI ASSOCIATION 1901

Curator
Mariano Efron,
Architecturestudio

Participants
Laureates and nominees of
Young European Architects
competition, selected by an
international jury

Website
www.ca-asi.com

Functioning as a laboratory, CA' ASI aims to make professional urban and architectural debates accessible to the public. It also promotes dialogue between contemporary architecture and art and between architects and artists of different generations and nationalities in order to question urban planning and architecture topics.

CA' ASI has been participating in the Biennale for the last ten years. It has successfully organised and featured the outcome of the following international architectural competitions: Young Chinese Architecture in 2010, Young Arab Architects in 2012, Young Architects in Africa in 2014, and Young Architects in Latin America in 2018.

On the occasion of the 17th International Architecture Exhibition, CA' ASI opens its doors to emerging European architects in order to highlight and identify their creativity and dynamics in today's architectural scene. This exhibition is a unique opportunity to underline the important role played by European architects, reflected by the renewal of their work. The present projects were selected by an international jury through a call for project that was amply publicised in Europe.

In our fragile planet, CA' ASI is sensitive to emerging topics and aims to promote an architecture of the future. In particular, it promotes energy transition, participatory habitation, the digital revolution, the circular economy, and imagination as responses to the rarefaction of resources.

Willem Hubrechts, *Off the Grid*, 2019.
Courtesy Fundació Mies van der Rohe

Monika Marinova, *Stage for the City*, 2019.
Courtesy Fundació Mies van der Rohe

JiSoo Kim, *Yulgok Street*, 2019.
Courtesy Fundació Mies van der Rohe

Shreeni Benjamin, *Mending the Gap*, 2019.
Courtesy Fundació Mies van der Rohe

Young Talent Architecture Award 2020. Educating together

FUNDACIÓ MIES VAN DER ROHE

The Young Talent Architecture Award (YTAA) aims to support the talent of recently graduated architects, urban planners, and landscape architects who will be responsible for transforming our environment in the future. YTAA emerged from curiosity about and interest in the initial stages in these students' development and a desire to support their talent as they enter the professional world.

YTAA was launched in 2016 and is open to all European architecture schools. In 2018, schools from China and South Korea were invited to participate as guest countries. In 2020, an independent edition was first organised with the four European Union Strategic Partners in Asia (China, India, Japan, and South Korea), aiming to promote exchange and cooperation with their YTAA counterparts in Europe and the 2020 guest countries (Brazil, Chile, and Mexico).

YTAA has thus become a platform to exchange knowledge on how we all learn architecture, and the exhibition speaks to how education in architecture can be undertaken together. The fact that many and very different architecture schools from all over the world participate and that representatives from other fields such as politicians and companies related to architecture also support the project makes it possible to organise an event with young architects and also other stakeholders (cultural managers, policy makers, representatives of companies...). In 2018, the jury highlighted that housing was a major topic and one of the Winners developed a project related to housing as well as some of the other finalists and shortlisted projects. The European Union Prize for Contemporary Architecture – Mies van der Rohe Award 2017 and 2019 Winners have dealt with housing, and YTAA 2020 also presents stimulating examples dealing with the concept of living together. The exhibition and the awards ceremony event highlight these aspects, which are perfectly in keeping with the aims of the 17th International Architecture Exhibition and the 2021 topic and title *How will we live toghether?*

Curators
Ivan Blasi
Anna Sala Giralt

Participants
Young Talent Architecture
    Award 2020 participants
Asia Edition of Young Talent
    Architecture Award 2020
    participants

Main partner
Creative Europe - European
    Commission

In Collaboration with
Architects' Council of Europe
European Association for
    Architectural Education
World Architects

With the Support of
European Cultural Centre
Jung
Jansen
Regent
USM

Websites
www.ytaaward.com
miesbcn.com

INDEX OF
PARTICIPANTS
2021
PARTICIPATING COUNTRIES
AND COLLATERAL EVENTS

ALBANIA
p. 7

Fiona Mali
Born in Shkodra, Albania, in 1992
She lives and works in Tirana,
Albania

Irola Andoni
Born in Korça, Albania, in 1988
She lives and works in Tirana,
Albania

Malvina Ferra
Born in Fier, Albania, in 1991
She lives and works in Tirana,
Albania

Rudina Breçani
Born in Tirana, Albania, in 1994
She lives and works in Tirana

Thomas Joseph Logoreci
Born in Monterey, California
(USA), in 1968
He lives and works in Tirana,
Albania

REPUBLIC OF ARMENIA
p. 11

INVIVIA
Founded in Cambridge, MA, USA,
in 1999
Allen Sayegh (Vosguerichian)
Stefano Andreani
Humbi Song
Isa Theresa He
www.invivia.com

Storaket Architectural Studio
p. 11
Founded in Yerevan, Armenia, in
2007
Meroujan Minassian
Narbeh Bedrossian
www.storaket.com

AUSTRIA
p. 15

Centre for Global Architecture

Vienna, Austria
www.globalarchitecture.org

REPUBLIC OF AZERBAIJAN
p. 17

Nariman Memarlig - Architectural
Studio
Founded in Baku, Azerbaijan, 2001
Established in Baku, Azerbaijan
http://narimanmemarliq.com/en/
home

Yakov Khalip
St. Petersburg, Russia, 1908 –
Moscow, Russia, 1980

Rashad Alakbarov
Born in Baku, Azerbaijan, in 1979
Lives and works in Baku, Azerbaijan

KINGDOM OF BAHRAIN
p. 19

Bas Smets
Born in Hasselt, Belgium, in 1975
He lives and works in Brussels,
Belgium, and Paris, France
www.bassmets.be

Anne Holtrop
Born in Tiels, the Netherlands, in
1977
She works and lives in Muharraq,
Bahrain
www.anneholtrop.nl

Christian Kerez
Born in Maracaibo, Venezuela, in
1962
He works and lives in Berlin,
Germany, and Zurich, Switzerland
www.kerez.ch

Pearling Path team
Founded in Muharraq, Bahrain, in
2009
www.pearlingpath.bh

OFFICE Kersten Geers David Van
Severen
Kersten Geers

Born in Ghent, Belgium, in 1975
David Van Severen
Born in Ghent, Belgium, in 1978
They work and live in Brussels,
Belgium
www.officekgdvs.com

Gionata Rizzi
Born in Milan, Italy, in 1961
He works and lives in Milan
www.studiogionatarizzi.com

Valerio Olgiati
Born in Chur, Switzerland, in 1958
He works and lives in Flims,
Switzerland
www.olgiati.net

BELGIUM
p. 21

360 Architecten bvba
Kris Buyse
Greet Houben
Jan Mannaerts
www.office360.be

Architecten Broekx-Schiepers
Jo Broekx
Marcella Schiepers
www.broekx-schiepers.be

Architecten De Vylder Vinck
Taillieu
Jan De Vylder
Inge Vinck
Jo Taillieu
www.architectendvvt.com

Architecten Els Claessens En Tania
Vandenbussche
Els Claessens
Tania Vandenbussche
Www.ectv.be

Architectenbureau Bart Dehaene
Bart Dehaene
www.bartdehaene.be

Arjaan De Feyter
www.arjaandefeyter.be

Baeten Hylebos Architecten
Evelyne Baeten

Jonas Hylebos
www.baetenhylebos.be

BLAF architecten
Bart Vanden Driessche
Lieven Nijs
www.blaf.be

Bovenbouw Architectuur
Dirk Somers
www.bovenbouw.be

BULK architecten
Johan Peeters
Koen Van Bockstal
Tom Vermeylen
www.bulkarchitecten.be

Collectief Noord Architecten
Pieter Eeckeloo
Christopher Paesbrugghe
Hans Van Bavel
Erik Wieërs
Peter Wills
www.collectiefnoord.be

COUSSÉE & GORIS architecten
Ralf Coussée
Klaas Goris
www.coussee-goris.com

De Smet Vermeulen architecten
Henk De Smet
Paul Vermeulen
www.hdspv.be

Dhooge & Meganck Architectuur
David Dhooge
Saar Meganck
www.dhoogemeganck.be

Dierendonckblancke architecten
Isabelle Blancke
Alexander Dierendonck
www.dierendonckblancke.eu

DMT architecten
Giedo Driesen
Jan Meersman
Jan Thomaes
www.dmtarchitecten.be

Doorzon interieurarchitecten
Stefanie Everaert
Caroline Lateur
www.doorzon.be

dmvA
David Driesen
Tom Verschueren
www.dmva-architecten.be

Eagles of Architecture
Bart Hollanders
www.eaglesofarchitecture.com

FELT architecture & design
Jasper Stevens
Karel Verstraeten
www.felt.works

GRAUX & BAEYENS architecten
Koen Baeyens
Basile Graux
www.graux-baeyens.be

HUB
Bart Biermans
Koen Drossaert
www.hub.eu

Marie-José Van Hee
www.mjvanhee.be

META architectuurbureau
Niklaas Deboutte
Eric Soors
www.meta.be

murmuur architecten
Koen Van Delsen
Pieter Vanderhoydonck
Tinne Verwerft
www.murmuur.eu

OFFICE Kersten Geers David Van
Severen
Kersten Geers
David Van Severen
www.officekgdvs.com

ono architectuur
Jonas Lindekens
Gert Somers
www.ono-architectuur.be

Poot Architectuur
Sarah Poot
www.poot-architectuur.be

PULS architecten
Philippe Van Deyck
Bram Vangampelaere

Bart Viellefont
www.pulsarchitecten.be

Raamwerk
Gijs De Cock
Freek Dendooven
www.raam-werk.com

Robbrecht en Daem architecten
Hilde Daem
Johannes Robbrecht
Paul Robbrecht
www.robbrechtendaem.com

Dierendonckblancke architecten
dierendonckblancke.eu

Schenk Hattori Architecture
Atelier
Daisuke Hattori
Steven Schenk
www.schenkhattori.com

Stéphane Beel Architects
Stéphane Beel
www.stephanebeel.com

Studiolo architectuur
Koen Matthys
Johan Liekens
Karolien Vanmerhaeghe
Sigyn De Lombaerde
www.studioloarchitectuur.be

Tim Peeters
www.timpeeters.eu

Tim Rogge Architectuur Studio
Anja Houbaert
Tim Rogge
Zoë Vanderstraeten
www.timrogge.be

Tom Thys
www.tomthysarchitecten.be

TRANS architectuur stedenbouw
Bram Aerts
Carolien Pasmans
www.transarchitectuurstedenbouw.be

TV AgwA – Ferrière
Benoît Burquel
Harold Fallon
Benoît Vandenbulcke
www.agwa.be

URA
Yves Malysse
Kiki Verbeeck
www.ura.be

Van Gelder Tilleman architects
Peter Van Gelder
Saar Tilleman
www.vangeldertilleman.be

Vermeiren – De Coster Architecten
Johan De Coster
Lieve Vermeiren
www.vdca.be

VERS.A ARCHITECTURE
Guillaume Becker
Kobe Van Praet
www.versa-architecture.be

Frederic Vandoninck Wouter
Willems architecten
Dennis Tyfus
Frederic Vandoninck
Wouter Willems
www.fvww.be

BRAZIL
p. 23

Luiza Baldan
Born in Rio de Janeiro, Brazil, in
1980
She lives and works in Berlin,
Germany

Gustavo Minas
Born in Cássia, Brazil, in 1981
He lives and works in Brasilia, Brazil

Joana França
Born in Brasilia, Brazil, in 1980
She lives and works in Brasilia,
Brazil

Amir Admoni
Born in São Paulo, Brazil, in 1977
He lives and works in São Paulo,
Brazil

Leonardo Finotti
Born in Uberlândia, Brazil, in 1977
He lives and works in São Paulo,
Brazil

Alexandre Delijaicov
Born in São Paulo, Brazil, in 1962
He lives and works in São Paulo

Aiano Bemfica
Born in Belo Horizonte, Brazil, 1986
He lives and works in Belo
Horizonte, Brazil

Cris Araújo
Born in Belo Horizonte, Brazil, in
1996
He lives and works in Belo
Horizonte, Brazil

Edinho Vieira
Born in Belo Horizonte, Brazil, in
1994
He lives and works in Belo
Horizonte, Brazil

CANADA
p. 25

T B A / Thomas Balaban Architect
Founded in Montreal, Canada, in
2009
t--b--a.com

PEOPLE'S REPUBLIC OF CHINA
p. 29

Zhu Zheqin (Dadawa)
Born in Guangzhou, People's
Republic of China, in 1968

He Wanyu
Born in Sichuan, People's Republic
of China, in 1983
She lives and works in Shenzhen,
People's Republic of China

Cui Kai
Born in Beijing, People's Republic of
China, in 1957
He lives and works in Beijing

Chang Qing
Born in Xi'an, People's Republic of
China, in 1957
He lives and works in Shanghai,
People's Republic of China

Zhuang Weimin
Born in Shanghai, People's Republic
of China, in 1962
He lives and works in Beijing,
People's Republic of China

Zhou Kai
Born in Tianjin, People's Republic
of China, in 1962
He lives and works in Tianjin

Liu Jiakun
Born in Chengdu, People's Republic
of China, in 1956
He lives and works in Chengdu

Xiao Wei
Born in Linjian, People's Republic of
China, in 1964
He lives and works in Wuhan,
People's Republic of China

CITIC General Institute of
Architectural Design and Research
Co. (CADI) Founded in Wuhan,
People's Republic of China, in 1952
www.whadi.citic.com

Lyu Zhou
Born in Beijing, People's Republic of
China, in 1959
He lives and works in Beijing

Liu Chang
Born in Beijing, People's Republic of
China, in 1968
He lives and works in Beijing

Zhao Peng
Born in Shenyang, People's
Republic of China, in 1977
He lives and works in Beijing,
People's Republic of China

Michele Bonino
Born in Torino, Italy, in 1974
He lives and works in Torino

Politecnico di Torino
Founded in Torino, Italy, in 1859
Established in Torino, Italy, in 1906
China Room Research Group
www.chinaroom.polito.it

Chen Xiong
Born in Guangzhou, People's

Republic of China, in 1962
He lives and works in Guangzhou

Cui Tong
Born in Beijing, People's Republic of
China, in 1962
He lives and works in Beijing

Dong Gong
Born in Beijing, People's Republic of
China, in 1972
He lives and works in Beijing

Gui Xuewen
Born in Wuhan, People's Republic
of China, in 1963
He lives and works in Wuhan

Guo Mingzhuo
Born in Shanghai, People's Republic
of China, in 1943
He lives and works in Guangzhou,
People's Republic of China

Hu Yue
Born in Beijing, People's Republic of
China, in 1964
He lives and works in Beijing

Li Cundong
Born in Dandong, People's Republic
of China, in 1971
Currently lives and works in Beijing,
People's Republic of China

Open Studio
Founded in New York, USA, in
2003, and in Beijing, People's
Republic of China, in 2008
Li Hu
Huang Wenjing
www.openarch.com

Li Xinggang
Born in Tangshan, People's
Republic of China, in 1969
He lives and works in Beijing,
People's Republic of China

Doreen Heng Liu
Born in Guangzhou, People's
Republic of China
She lives and works in Shenzhen and
Hong Kong, People's Republic of
China

Liu Xiaodu
Born in Beijing, People's Republic of
China, in 1961
He lives and works in Shenzhen,
People's Republic of China, and
Beijing

Atelier Deshaus
Founded in Shanghai, People's
Republic of China, in 2001
Liu Yichun
Chen Yifeng

Gisela Loehlein
Born in Schwaebisch Hall,
Germany, in 1971
She lives and works in Hangzhou,
People's Republic of China

Xi'an Jiaotong – Liverpool
University (XJTLU)
Established in Hangzhou, People's
Republic of China, in 2006
www.xjtlu.edu.cn

Lyu Pinjing
Born in Fengcheng, People's
Republic of China, in 1966
He lives and works in Beijing,
People's Republic of China

Ma Yansong
Born in Beijing, People's Republic of
China, in 1975
He lives and works in Beijing and
Los Angeles, USA

Mei Hongyuan
Born in Yingkou, People's Republic
of China, in 1958
He lives and works in Harbin,
People's Republic of China

Meng Yan
Born in Beijing, People's Republic of
China, in 1964
He lives and works in Shenzhen,
People's Republic of China, and
Beijing

Ni Yang
Born in Beijing, People's Republic of
China, in 1963
He lives and works in Guangzhou,
People's Republic of China

Qi Xin
Born in Beijing, People's Republic of
China, in 1959
He lives and works in Beijing

Shen Di
Born in Shanghai, People's Republic
of China, in 1960
He lives and works in Shanghai

Shen Zuowei
Born in Shandong, People's
Republic of China, in 1963
He lives and works in Jinan, People's
Republic of China

Song Zhaoqing
Born in Leshan, People's Republic
of China, in 1970
He lives and works in Shanghai

Sun Yimin
Born in Hohhot, People's Republic
of China, in 1964
He lives and works in Guangzhou,
People's Republic of China

Wang Hui
Born in Beijing, People's Republic of
China, in 1967
He lives and works in Beijing

Wang Xiao'an
Born in Shanghai, People's Republic
of China, in 1953
He lives and works in Shanghai

Yang Ying
Born in Hunan, People's Republic of
China, in 1964
He lives and works in Hunan

Zhang Jie
Born in Jinan, China in 1963
He lives and works in Beijing,
People's Republic of China

Zhang Ming
Born in Wuxi, People's Republic of
China, in 1968
He lives and works in Shanghai,
People's Republic of China

Zhang Pengju
Born in Inner Mongolia, People's
Republic of China, in 1963

He lives and works in Inner Mongolia

Zhang Tong
Born in Hangzhou, People's Republic of China, in 1969
Currently lives and works in Nanjing, People's Republic of China

Zhang Yue
Born in Hunan, People's Republic of China, in 1973
He lives and works in Beijing, People's Republic of China

Zhao Yang
Born in Chongqing, People's Republic of China, in 1980
He lives and works in Dali, People's Republic of China

Zhao Yuanchao
Born in Xi'an, People's Republic of China, in 1963
He lives and works in Xi'an

Zhu Xiaodi
Born in Beijing, People's Republic of China, in 1964
He lives and works in Beijing

CROATIA
p. 31

Davor Mišković
Born in Rijeka, Croatia, in 1971
He lives and works in Rijeka

Ida Križaj Leko
Born in Zagreb, Croatia, in 1983
She lives and works in Rijeka, Croatia

Ivan Dorotić
Born in Split, Croatia, in 1980
He lives and works between Croatia and Berlin, Germany

Leo Kirinčić
Born in Rijeka, Croatia, in 1988
He lives and works in Rijeka

Ana-Marija (Maša) Poljanec
Born in Zagreb, Croatia, in 1983

She lives and works in Zagreb

Renato Stankovi
Born in Rijeka, Croatia, in 1987
He lives and works in Croatia

Morana Matković
Born in Zagreb, Croatia, in 1985
She lives and works in Rijeka, Croatia, and Zagreb

Jana Horvat
Born in Zagreb, Croatia, in 1993
She lives and works in Zagreb

DENMARK
p. 35

Lundgaard & Tranberg Architects
Founded in Copenhagen, Denmark, in 1985
Boje Lundgaard
Lene Tranberg
Erik Frandsen
Benjamin Ter-Borch
Julius Nielsen
Henrik Schmidt
Signe Baadsgaard
Mikkel Kjærgård Christiansen
www.ltarkitekter.dk

DOMINICAN REPUBLIC
p. 37

Lidia León Cabral
Born in Santo Domingo, Dominican Republic, in 1962
She lives and works between Santo Domingo and Montreal, Canada

EGYPT
p. 39

Mostafa Rabea Abdelbaset
Born in Egypt in 1978
He lives and works in Lebanon

Mohamad Riad Alhalaby
Born in Lebanon in 1993
He lives and works in Lebanon

Amr Allam
Born in Egypt in 1991
He lives and works in Egypt

Ahmed Essam
Born in Egypt in 1993
He lives and works in Egypt

GREAT BRITAIN
p. 49

Unscene Architecture
Founded in London, UK, in 2019
Manijeh Verghese
Madeleine Kessler
www.unscenearchitecture.com

The Decorators
www.the-decorators.net

Studio Polpo
www.studiopolpo.it

Public Works
www.publicworksgroup.net

vPPR Architects
Founded in London, UK, in 2009
Tatiana von Preussen
Catherine Pease
Jessica Reynolds
vppr.co.uk

GREECE
p. 51

Nikos Kalogirou
Born in Veria, Greece, in 1951
He lives and works in Thessaloniki, Greece

Themis Chatzigiannopoulos
Born in in Thessaloniki, Greece, in 1984
He lives and works in Thessaloniki, Greece

Maria Dousi
Born in Athens, Greece, in 1962
She lives and works in Thessaloniki, Greece

Dimitrios G. Kontaxakis
Born in Thessaloniki, Greece, in 1968
He lives and works in Thessaloniki, Greece

Sofoklis Kotsopoulos
Born in Florina, Greece, in 1982
He lives and works in Thessaloniki, Greece

Dimitris Thomopoulos
Born in Athens, Greece, in 1974
He lives and works in Thessaloniki, Greece

GRENADA
p. 53

Bryan W. Bullen
Born in St. Andrew, Grenada, in 1966
He works in St. George's, Grenada

Caribbean office of Co-operative Architecture (COCOA)
Established in St. George's Grenada, 2000
www.cocoa.gd

HUNGARY
p. 55

A-A Collective
Established in Warsaw, Poland, 2018.
www.a-a-collective.com
Zygmunt Borawski
Born in Bagno a Ripoli, Italy, in 1987
He lives and works in Warsaw, Poland
Martin Marker Larsen
Born in Kalundborg, Denmark, in 1987
He lives and works in Copenhagen, Denmark
Furio Montoli
Born in Nagoya, Japan, in 1989
He lives and works in Basel, Switzerland
Srdjan Zlokapa
Born in Sarajevo, Yugoslavia, 1989

He lives and works in Basel, Switzerland

Architecture Uncomfortable Workshop
Established in Budapest, Hungary, in 2012
auworkshop.com
Emil Dénes Ghyczy
Born in Budapest, Hungary, in 1984
He lives and works in Budapest
Lukács Szederkényi
Born in Budapest, Hungary, in 1983
He lives and works in Budapest
Anna, Zsoldos
Born in Nagykanizsa, Hungary, in 1995
She lives and works in Budapest, Hungary

b210
Established in Tallinn, Estonia, in 2012
www.b210.ee
Aet Ader
Born in Tallinn, Estonia, in 1985
She lives and works in Tallinn
Karin Tõugu
Born in Tallinn, Estonia, in 1985
She lives and works in Tallinn
Mari Hunt
Born in Tallinn, Estonia, in 1986
She lives and works in Tallinn
Kadri Klementi
Born in Tallinn, Estonia, in 1984
She lives and works in Tallinn
Mari Mõldre
Born in Tallinn, Estonia, 1992
She lives and works in Tallinn
Arvi Anderson
Born in Rapla, Estonia, in 1992
He lives and works in Tallinn, Estonia
Nele Sverns
Born in Tallinn, Estonia, in 1989
She lives and works in Tallinn

Budcud
Established in Cracow, Poland, in 2011
budcud.org
Mateusz Adamczyk
Born in Katowice, Poland, in 1981
He lives and works in Cracow, Poland
Agata Woźniczka

Born in Wrocław, Poland, in 1986
She lives and works in Cracow, Poland

Konntra
Established in Portorož, Slovenia; Skopje, North Macedonia; Zagreb, Croatia in 2018
konntra.com
Erik Jurišević
Born in Koper, Slovenia, 1993
He lives and works in Portorož, Slovenia
Mirjana Lozanovska
Born in Skopje, North Macedonia, in 1992
She lives and works in Skopje, North Macedonia
Silvija Shaleva
Born in Skopje, North Macedonia, in 1993
She lives and works in Zagreb, Croatia

Mada
Established in Belgrade, Serbia, in 2013
www.mada.rs
Nikola Andonov
Born in Belgrade, Serbia, in 1986
He lives and works in Belgrade
Stefan Stojanović
Born in Niš, Serbia, in 1988
He lives and works in Belgrade, Serbia
Aleksandar Ristović
Born in Užice, Serbia, in 1987
He lives and works in Belgrade, Serbia

MNPL Workshop
Established in Odessa, Ukraine in 2009
Viktor Prokhorov
Born in Odessa, Ukraine, in 1986
He lives and works in Odessa
Eugene Prokhorov
Born in Odessa, Ukraine, in 1986
He lives and works in Odessa
Oleksiy Bilokurenko
Born in Odessa, Ukraine, in 1986
He lives and works in Odessa
Denis Flora
Born in Odessa, Ukraine, in 1986
He lives and works in Odessa
Oleg Kovalenko

Born in Odessa, Ukraine, in 1987
He lives and works in Odessa
Ilya Soldatov
Born in Odessa, Ukraine, in 1983
He lives and works in Odessa
Olekiy Mykhailov
Born in Odessa, Ukraine, in 1989
He lives and works in Kiev, Ukraine
Marila Kovtiushenko
Born in Odessa, Ukraine, in 1989
She lives and works in Kiev, Ukraine

Paradigma Ariadné
Established in Budapest, Hungary, in 2016
paradigmaariadne.com
Dávid Smiló
Born in Budapest, Hungary, in 1988
He lives and works in Budapest
Szabolcs Molnár
Born in Szeged, Hungary, in 1989
He lives and works in Budapest, Hungary
Attila Róbert Csóka
Born in Zilah, Romania, in 1988
He lives and works in Budapest, Hungary

Plural
Established in Bratislava, Slovakia, in 2009
Martin Jančok
Born in Presov, Slovakia, in 1978
He lives and works in Bratislava, Slovakia
Michal Janák
Born in Bratislava, Slovakia, in 1987
He lives and works in Bratislava

Vojtěch Rada
Established in Prague, Czech Republic, in 2013
www.vojtechrada.com
Vojtěch Rada
Born in Prague, Czech Republic, in 1991
He lives and works in Prague

RLOALUARNAD
Established in London, United Kingdom, in 2016
www.rloaluarnad.com
Roland Reemaa
Born in Pärnu, Estonia, in 1987
He lives and works in London, United Kingdom

Laura Linsi
Born in Tallinn, Estonia, in 1989
She lives and works in London, United Kingdom

Studio Act
Established in Bucharest, Romania, in 1999
www.studio-act.com
Horia Spirescu
Born in Bucharest, Romania, 1987
He lives and works in Bucharest
Atanasiu Alexandru
Born in Bucharest, Romania, in 1986
He lives and works in Bucharest
Wanda Hutira
Born in Baia Mare, Romania, 1985
She lives and works in Bucharest, Romania
Victor Serbanescu
Born in Slobozia, Romania, in 1993
He lives and works in Bucharest, Romania
Vlad Iosif
Born in Targoviste, Romania, in 1990
He lives and works in Bucharest, Romania
Dragos Raicu
Born in Bucharest, Romania, in 1986
He lives and works in Bucharest
Alexandra Albu
Born in Bucharest, Romania, in 1989
She lives and works in Bucharest

IRAQ
p. 57

Safina Projects CIC
Established in London, UK, in 2017, with fieldwork in Iraq
www.safinaprojects.org

Edge of Arabia
Established in London, UK, in 2003
www.edgeofarabia.com

Rashad Salim
Born in Khartoum, Sudan, in 1957
He lives and works in London, UK; Baghdad, Basra, and field locations, Iraq

IRELAND
p. 59

Annex

Sven Anderson
Born in Boston, USA, in 1977
He lives and works in Dublin,
Ireland
www.svenanderson.net
Alan Butler
Born in Dublin, Ireland in 1981
He lives and works in Dublin
www.alanbutler.info
David Capener
Born in Gloucester, UK in 1976
He lives and works in Dublin,
Ireland and Belfast, Northern
Ireland
www.davidcapener.com
Fiona McDermott
Born in Galway, Ireland in 1982
She lives and works in Dublin,
Ireland
www.fionamcdermott.org
Donal Lally
Born in Dublin, Ireland in 1981
He lives and works in Dublin
www.z-dm.com
Clare Lyster
Born in Ireland in 1970
She lives and works in Chicago, USA
www.cluaa.com

ISRAEL
p. 61

Dan Hasson
Born in Jerusalem, Israel, in 1974
He lives and works in Tel-Aviv,
Israel

Iddo Ginat
Born in Tel Aviv, Israel, in 1973
He lives and works in Tel-Aviv,
Israel

Rachel Gottesman
Born in Tel Aviv, Israel, in 1976
She lives and works in Tel-Aviv,
Israel

Yonatan Cohen
Born in Rehovot, Israel, in 1977

He lives and works in Pardes Hana,
Israel

Tamar Novick
Born in Ashkelon, Israel, in 1981
She lives and works in Berlin,
Germany

Netta Laufer
Born in Jerusalem, Israel, in 1986
She lives and works in Tel Aviv,
Israel

Shadi Habib Allah
Born in Nazareth, Israel, in 1985
He lives and works in Ein mahel,
Israel

Noa Yafe
Born in Yafo, Israel, in 1978
She lives and works in Tel Aviv,
Israel

Daniel Meir
Born in Haifa, Israel, in 1972
He lives and works in Tel Aviv, Israel

Apollo Legisamo
Born in Valencia, Venezuela, in
1968
He lives and works in Tel Aviv, Israel

JAPAN
p. 69

Jo Nagasaka
Born in Osaka, Japan, in 1971
He lives and works in Tokyo, Japan
schemata.jp

Ryoko Iwase
Born in Niigata, Japan, in 1984
She lives and works in Tokyo and
Kyoto, Japan
www.ryokoiwase.com

Toshikatsu Kiuchi
Born in Tokyo, Japan, in 1978
He lives and works in Tokyo, Japan
www.toshikatsukiuchi.com

Taichi Sunayama
Born in Kyoto, Japan, in 1980
He lives in Tokyo, works in Tokyo

and Kyoto, Japan
tsnym.nu/studio

Daisuke Motogi
Born in Saitama, Japan, in 1981
He lives and works in Tokyo, Japan
dskmtg.com

Rikako Nagashima
Born in Ibaraki, Japan, in 1980
She lives and works in Tokyo, Japan
rikako-nagashima.com

LATVIA
p. 77

NRJA
Established in Riga, Latvia in 2005
www.nrja.lv

LEBANON
p. 79

Paul Virilio
Born in Paris, France in 1932
He lives and works in Paris

Etel Adnan
Born in Beirut, Lebanon in 1925
She lives and works in Paris

LITHUANIA
p. 81

Julijonas Urbonas
Born in Klaipėda, Lithuania, in 1981
He lives and works in Vilnius,
Lithuania

GRAND DUCHY OF
LUXEMBOURG
p. 83

LUCA Luxembourg Center for
Architecture
Established in Luxembourg City,
Luxembourg in 1992
www.luca.lu

REPUBLIC OF NORTH
MACEDONIA
p. 85

Bekir Ademi
Born in Gostivar, North Macedonia
in 1980
He lives and works in Skopje, North
Macedonia

Jordan Šišovski
Born in Skopje, Macedonia
(Yugoslavia) in 1978
He lives and works in Skopje

Ana Rafailovska
Born in Skopje, North Macedonia
in 1983
She lives and works in Skopje

Amine Ademi
Born in Skopje, North Macedonia
in 1988
She lives and works in Skopje

Enis Abovski
Born in Tetovo, Macedonia in 1994
He lives and works in Skopje, North
Macedonia

Atanas Naumovski
Born in Skopje, North Macedonia
in 1983
He lives and works in Skopje

Enes Sever
Born in Istanbul, Turkey in 1993
He lives and works in Rotterdam,
Netherlands

Dren Nevzati
Born in Prizren, Kosovo in 1989
He lives and works in Skopje, North
Macedonia

Gavril Boshkovski
Born in Prilep, North Macedonia
in 1995
He lives and works in Skopje, North
Macedonia

Elmedina Hasani
Born in Skopje, North Macedonia
in 1995
He lives and works in Skopje

Nita Çavoli
Born in Skopje, North Macedonia
in 1980
He lives and works in Skopje

Aida Bakalli Salihu
Born in Gjakova, Kosovo in 1992
He lives and works in Skopje, North
Macedonia

Ivana Chalovska
Born in Ohrid, North Macedonia
in 1992
She lives and works in Skopje,
North Macedonia

MONTENEGRO
p. 89

Vasilija Abramović
Born in Podgorica, Montenegro in
1990
She lives and works in London, UK

Ruairi Glynn
Born in London, UK in 1981
He lives and works in London

Parker Heyl
Born in North Haven, Connecticut
in 1993
He lives and works in London

THE NETHERLANDS
p. 91

Afaina de Jong
She lives and works in Amsterdam,
the Netherlands

Debra Solomon
She lives and works in Amsterdam,
the Netherlands

Website
biennale2020.hetnieuweinstituut.nl

NORDIC COUNTRIES
NORWAY-SWEDEN-FINLAND
p. 93

Helen & Hard AS
Founded in Stavanger, Norway,
1996
Established in Stavanger, Norway
and Oslo, Norway
www.helenhard.no

Anna Ihle
Born in Stavanger, Norway 1984
She lives and works in Stavanger,
Norway

PAKISTAN
p. 95

Sara M. Anwar
Born in Dhahran, Saudi Arabia in
1979
She lives and works in Dubai,
United Arab Emirates

Madeeha Yasin Merchant
Born in Abu Dhabi, United Arab
Emirates in 1983
She lives and works in New York,
USA

Farhan Anwar
Born in Karachi, Pakistan in 1968
He lives and works in Karachi

Shama Dossa
Born in Prince George BC, Canada
in 1976
She lives and works in Karachi
Pakistan

Hira Zuberi
Born in Karachi, Pakistan in 1990
She lives and works in Karachi

PHILIPPINES
p. 99

Framework Collaborative
Alexander Eriksson Furunes
Born in Trondheim, Norway, in
1988.

He lives and works in Norway and
Philippines.
www.erikssonfurunes.com
Sudarshan V. Khadka Jr.
Born in Manila, Philippines, in
1986.
He lives and works in Manila.
www.iincite.design
GK Enchanted Farm Community
Established in Angat, Bulacan,
Philippines, in 2010

PORTUGAL
p. 103

Artéria
Founded in Lisbon, Portugal, in 2011
www.arteria.pt

Ateliermob
Founded in Lisbon, Portugal, in
2005
www.ateliermob.com

Barbas Lopes Arquitectos
Founded in Lisbon, Portugal, in
2006
www.barbaslopes.com

Cerejeira Fontes Architects
Founded in Braga, Portugal, in 1996
cerejeirafontesarchitects.com

Colectivo Warehouse
Founded in Lisbon, Portugal, in
2013
www.warehouse.pt

Habitar Porto
Founded in Oporto, in 2016
habitarporto.org

Laboratório de Habitação Básica
(LAHB)
Founded in Oporto, Portugal, in
2013
lahb.pt

Manuel Graça Dias + Egas José
Vieira Arquitectos
Founded in Lisbon, Portugal, in
1990
www.contemporanea.com.pt

meerooficina
Founded in Oporto, Portugal, in
2014
www.meerooficina.com

Alexandre Alves Costa
Born in Oporto, Portugal, in 1939
He lives and works in Oporto

Alexandre Dias
Born in Oporto, Portugal, in 1974
He lives and works in Coimbra,
Portugal

Álvaro Siza
Born in Oporto, Portugal, in 1933
He lives and works in Oporto
www.sizavieira.pt

Ana Luísa Rodrigues
Born in Lourenço Marques,
Mozambique, in 1969
She lives in Oporto and works in
Guimarães, Portugal

Bruno Silvestre
Born in Sintra, Portugal, in 1974
He lives and works in London,
Great Britain

Charles Cossement
Born in Tournai, Belgium, in 1992
He lives and works in Lisbon,
Portugal

Egas José Vieira
Born in Lisbon, Portugal, in 1962
Lives and works in Lisbon

Fernando Seabra-Santos
Born in Coimbra, Portugal, in 1955
He lives in Coimbra

Francisco da Conceição Silva
Lisbon, Portugal 1922 - Brasil, 1982
He lived and worked in Lisbon

Francisco Pereira
Born in Figueira da Foz, Portugal,
in 1991
He lives and works in Oporto,
Portugal

Frederico Eça
Born in Oporto, Portugal, in 1973
He lives and works in Oporto

Gil Cardoso
Born in Lisbon, Portugal, in 1992
He lives and works in Lisbon

Inês Beleza de Azevedo
Born in Oporto, Portugal, in 1991
She lives and works in Oporto

João Archer de Carvalho
Born in Oporto, Portugal, in 1928

João Figueira
Born in Figueira da Foz, Portugal,
in 1968
He lives and works in Lisbon,
Portugal

João Pernão
Born in Lisbon, Portugal, in 1963
He lives and works in Lisbon

João Siopa Alves
Born in Alcobaça, Portugal, in 1992
He lives and works in Lisbon,
Portugal

José Barra
Born in Lisbon, Portugal, in 1966
He lives and works in Lisbon

José Gigante
Born in Oporto, Portugal, in 1952
He lives and works in Oporto

José Lobo Almeida
Born in Oporto, Portugal, in 1981
He lives and works in Oporto

José Miguel Rodrigues
Born in Oporto, Portugal, in 1970
He lives and works in Oporto

José Neves
Born in Lisbon, Portugal, in 1963
He lives and works in Lisbon

José Santa Bárbara
Born in Lisbon, Portugal, in 1936
He lives and works in Sintra,
Portugal

José Veloso
Born in Lagos, Portugal, in 1930
He lives and works in Lagos

Luís Miguel Fareleira
Born in Oporto, Portugal, in 1971
He lives and works in Bangkok,
Thailand

Luís Spranger
Born in Johannesburg, South Africa,
in 1972
He lives and works in Ponta do Sol,
Madeira, Portugal

Manuel Teles
Coimbra, Portugal, 1936 – Oporto,
Portugal , 2012
He lived and worked in Oporto

Margarida Carvalho
Born in Oporto, Portugal, in 1982
She lives and works in Oporto

Maria Vale
Born in Lisbon, Portugal, in 1992
She lives and works in Lisbon

Nunes de Almeida
Oporto, Portugal, 1924 – 2014

Nuno Valentim
Born in Oporto, Portugal, in 1971
He lives and works in Oporto

Paulo Moreira
Born in Oporto, Portugal, in 1980
He lves and works in Oporto

Pedro Bandeira
Born in Barcelos, Portugal, in 1970
He lives in Oporto and works in
Guimarães, Portugal

Pedro Brígida
Born in Coimbra, Portugal, in 1969
He lives and works in Coimbra
www.pedrobrigida.com

Rita Dourado
Born in Lisbon, Portugal, in 1973
She lives and works in Lisbon

Rogério Ramos
Oporto, Portugal, 1927 – 1976

Sérgio Fernandez
Born in Oporto, Portugal, in 1937
He lives and works in Oporto

Sofia Augusto
Born in Pinhel, Portugal, in 1985
She lives and works in Oporto,
Portugal
sofiafaugusto.com

Tiago Baptista
Born in Lisbon, Portugal, in 1974
He lives in Oeiras and works in
Torres Vedras, Portugal

Vítor Figueiredo
Figueira da Foz, Portugal 1929 –
Lisbon, Portugal, 2004

ROMANIA
p. 105

Ideilagram
Founded in 2016. Based in
Bucharest, Romania
www.ideilagram.ro

Teleleu
Founded in 2013.
Conducts its research around
Europe from a minivan
https://teleleu.eu/

Mazzocchioo
Founded in 2017.
Based in Bucharest, Romania
www.mazzocchioo.com

REPUBLIC OF SAN MARINO
p. 109

Fan Haimin
Born in Shanghai, China, in 1959.
Lives and works in Beijing, China

Fu Yuxiang
Born in Chongqing, China, in 1963.
Lives and works in Chongqing

Min Yiming
Born in Fujian Province, China, in
1957.
Lives and works in Xia Men, China

NIE Jingzhu
Born in Beijing, China, in 1980.

Shen Jingdong
Born in Nanjing, Jiangsu, China, in
1965.
Lives and works in Beijing, China

Wang Yi
Born in Jiangsu, China, in 1960.
Lives and works in Beijing, China

Wu Wei 　ì
Born in Guang Dong Province,
China, in 1994

Zhang Zhaohong
Born in Beijing, China, in 1969
Lives and works in Beijing

Enrico Muscioni
Born in Bologna, Italy, in 1977

Massimiliano Raggi
Born in San Marino in 1967

Riccardo Varini
Born in Trieste, Italy, in 1968

SAUDI ARABIA
p. 111

Hussam Dakkak
Born in Jeddah, Saudi Arabia, in
1988
He lives and works in London,
United Kingdom

Basmah Kaki
Born in Laussane, Switzerland, in
1989
She lives and works in Jeddah, Saudi
Arabia

Hessa Al Bader
Born in Kuwait City, Kuwait, in
1989
She lives and works in Kuwait City

SERBIA
p. 113

MuBGD
was established in Belgrade, Serbia,
in 2018.

Iva Bekić was born in Zagreb, Yugoslavia, in 1987.
She lives and works in Belgrade, Serbia.

Petar Cigić was born in Novi Sad, Yugoslavia, in 1987.
He lives and works in Belgrade, Serbia.

Dalia Dukanac was born in Zagreb, Yugoslavia, in 1989.
She lives and works in Belgrade, Serbia.
Stefan Đorđević was born in Čačak, Yugoslavia, in 1987.
He lives and works in Belgrade, Serbia.
Irena Gajić was born in Belgrade, Yugoslavia, in 1987.
She lives and works in Belgrade, Serbia.
Mirjana Ješić was born in Pančevo, Yugoslavia, in 1988.
She lives and works in Belgrade, Serbia.
Hristina Stojanović was born in Belgrade, Yugoslavia, in 1991.
She lives and works in Belgrade, Serbia.
Snežana Zlatković was born in Belgrade, Yugoslavia, in 1988.
She lives and works in Belgrade, Serbia.

SINGAPORE
p. 115

Atelier HOKO
Established in Singapore, in 2002
www.atelierhoko.com

DP Architects
Established in Singapore, in 1967
www.dpa.com.sg

Drama Box
Established in Singapore, in 1990

ArtsWok Collaborative
Established in Singapore, in 2002

Forest & Whale
Established in Singapore, in 2006

Hyphen Architects + Brian Khoo + Mary Ann Ng
Established in Singapore, in 2015
www.hyphenarch.com

Imran bin Tajudeen
Born in Singapore.
Lives and works in Oxford, Great Britain

Lee Kah Hui
Born in Singapore.
She lives and works in Tokyo, Japan

Iqbal bin Roslan
Born in Singapore.
He lives and works in Singapore

Lai Chee Kien
Born in Singapore.
Lives and works in Singapore and Taiwan
www.laicheekien.com

Lighting Planners Associates
Established in Tokyo and Singapore
www.lighting.co.jp

Millennial Nomad Space
Established in Singapore in 2019
www.millennialnomadspace.com

MKPL Architects
Established in Singapore in 1995
www.mkpl.com.sg

NUS-Tsinghua Design Research Initiative: Sharing Cities
Established in Singapore and Beijing, China, in 2017
www.nt-drisc.org

Red Bean Architects
Established in Singapore in 2009
www.redbeanarch.com

salad dressing
Established in Singapore in 2002
www.saladlandscape.com

Studio Lapis
Established in Singapore in 2009
www.studiolapis.sg
Michael Budig
Born in Austria.
He lives and works in Singapore

Oliver Heckmann
Born in Münster, Germany.
He lives and works in Singapore

Singapore University of Technology and Design
Established in Singapore in 2009
www.asd.sutd.edu.sg

WOHA
Established in Singapore in 1994.
www.woha.net

SPAIN
p. 119

Sergio, Hernández Carretero
Born in Alicante, Spain, in 1981
Lives and works in Alicante, Spain
orsieg.es

Hyperstudio
Cristóbal, Baños Hernández
Born in Murcia, Spain, in 1995
He lives and works in Tokyo, Japan

Diego, Iglesias Gómez
Born in Madrid, Spain, in 1992
He lives and works in Tokyo, Japan
www.hyperstudio.es

Creus e Carrasco
Covadonga, Carrasco López
Born in Ribadeo, Spain, in 1965
She lives and works in A Coruña, Spain

Juan, Creus Andrade
Born in Cee, Spain, in 1966
He lives and works in A Coruña, Spain
www.creusecarrasco.com

Paisaje Transversal
Guillermo, Acero Caballero
Born in Madrid, Spain, in 1984
He lives and works in Madrid
Jon, Aguirre Such
Born in San Sebastian, Spain, in 1984
He lives and works in Madrid, Spain
Jorge, Arévalo Martín
Born in Madrid, Spain, in 1988
He lives and works in Madrid

Pilar, Díaz Rodríguez
Born in Valencia, Spain, in 1984
She lives and works in Valencia
Iñaki, Romero Fernández de Larrea
Born in Vitoria, Spain, in 1984
He lives and works in Valencia, Spain
www.paisajetransversal.com

Quatrecaps
Bernat, Ivars Vinaroz
Born in Denia, Spain, in 1981
He lives and works in Valencia, Spain

Dídac, Sendra Rabena
Born in Valencia Spain, in 1991
He lives and works in Valencia
Juan, Suay Rel
Born in Meliana Spain, in 1991
He lives and works in Valencia, Spain
Miguel, Tomás Tena
Born in Castellón de la Plana, Spain, in 1991
He lives and works in Valencia, Spain
wwwquatrecaps.com

Airlab
Carlos Bañón
Born in Alicante, Spain in 1978
He lives and works in Singapore

Félix Raspall
Born in Buenos Aires, Argentina, in 1979
He lives and works in Santiago de Chile, Chile

Joan, Margarit i Consarnau
Born in Sanahuja, Spain, in 1938
He lives and works in San Justo Desvern, Spain
www.joanmargarit.com

Recetas Urbanas
Santiago Cirugeda Parejo
Born in Sevilla, Spain, in 1971
He lives and works in Sevilla, Spain

Alice Attout
Born in Namur, Belgium, in 1984
She lives and works in Sevilla, Spain
www.recetasurbanas.net

Sawu Studio
Aylin Vera Ramos
Born in Iquique, Chile, in 1987
She lives and works in Madrid,
Spain
Pablo García Mena
Born in Madrid, Spain, in 1982
He lives and works in Madrid
www.sawustudio.com

Chiara Farinea
Born in San Donà di Piave, Italy, in
1979
She lives and works in Barcelona,
Spain

Mohamad El Atab
Born in Saida, Lebanon, in 1991
He lives and works in Barcelona,
Spain

Federica Ciccone
Born in Palmi, Italy, in 1987
She liives and works in Barcelona,
Spain

Sotiria Sarri
Born in Larissa, Greece, in 1989
She liives and works in Barcelona,
Spain
www.sotiriasarri.com

Contextos de Arquitectura
Óscar Miguel Ares
Born in Valladolid, Spain, in 1972
He lives and works in Valladolid
Javier Palomero Alonso
Born in Segovia, Spain, in 1976
He lives and works in Rivas-
Vaciamadrid, Spain
Bárbara Arranz González
Born in Valladolid, Spain, in 1978
Lives and works in Valladolid
Felipe Pou Chapa
Born in Pamplona, Spain, in 1987
He lives and works in Valladolid,
Spain
Carmen Gimeno Sanz
Born in Valladolid, Spain, in 1987
She lives and works in Valladolid
Eduardo Rodríguez Gallego
Born in Salamanca, Spain, in 1994
He lives and works in Valladolid,
Spain
Judit Sigüenza González
Born in Valladolid, Spain, in 1993

She lives and works in Valladolid
Luis Matas Royo
Born in Guijuelo, Spain, in 1993
He lives and works in Valladolid,
Spain
Jesús j. Ruíz Alonso
Born in Palencia, Spain, in 1988
He lives and works in Madrid, Spain
Dorota Tokarska
Born in Lublin, Poland, in 1989
She lives and works in Madrid,
Spain
Sergio Alonso Alonso
Born in Valladolid, Spain in 1993
He lives and works in Valladolid and
Barcelona, Spain
Iñaki Albistur Martín
Born in Donostia, Spain, in 1982
He lives and works in Donostia
Raquel M.Ares Joana
Born in Portugalete, Spain,in 1977
She lives and works in Donostia,
Spain
www.arquimaña.com

Miguel Arraiz García
Born in Valencia, Spain, in 1975
He lives and works in Valencia
www.miguelarraiz.com

David Moreno Terrón
Born in Torrent, Spain, in 1975
He lives and works in Valencia,
Spain

Rosa Gallardo Parralo
Born in Gibraleón, Spain, in 1989
She lives and works in Sevilla, Spain
www.rosagallardoparralo.berta.me

Macarena Castillo Párraga
Born in Jaén, Spain, in 1988
She lives and works in Málaga,
Spain

Araceli Calero Castro
Born in Pozoblanco, Spain, in 1989
She lives and works in Tolouse,
France
www.aracelicalero.com

Milena Villalba Montoya
Born in Valencia, Spain, in 1984
She lives and works in Valencia
www.milenavillalba.com

Santiago Hernández Puig
Born in Alicante, Spain, in 1989
He lives and works in Valencia, Spain
www.santihpuig.com

Pareid Studio
Déborah López Lobato
Born in Cacabelos, Spain, in 1987
She lives and works in London,
United Kingdom
Hadin Charbel
Born in Los Angeles, US, in 1987
He lives and works in London,
United Kingdom
www.pareid.com

John Porral Soldevilla
Born in Madrid, Spain, in 1987
He lives and works in Madrid
www.johnporral.com

Alberto López de Lucas
Born in Guadalajara, Spain, in 1992
He lives and works in Madrid, Spain
www.lopezdelucas.com

Animali Domestici
Alicia Lazzaroni
Born in Sanremo, Italy, in 1983
She lives and works in Bangkok,
Thailand
Antonio Bernacchi
Born in Gallarate, Italy, in 1983
He lives and works in Bangkok,
Thailand
www.animalidomestici.eu

MagicArch
María José Marcos Torró
Born in Alicante, Spain, in 1981
She lives and works in Murcia, Spain
and Seoul, South Korea
www.magicarch.es

FabLab Alicante
Set in Alicante, Spain
www.fablab.ua.es

FabLab Laboratorio de Artesanía
Digital [L.A.D.]
Set in San Pedro del Pinatar, Spain
www.laboratoriodeartesaniadigital.
com

Natoural DS
Carlos Timoner Lloréns

Born in Alicante, Spain, in 1982
He lives and works in Murcia, Spain
Juan Francisco Sánchez López
Born in Murcia. Spain, in 1988
He lives and works in Murcia and
Alicante, Spain
Juan Antonio García Navarro
Born in Murcia, Spain, in 1982
He lives and works in Sevilla, Spain
Pedro Milanés Hernández
Born in Murcia, Spain, in 1974
He lives and works in Murcia
Javier Torres Suárez
Born in Alicante, Spain, in 1982
He lives and works in Alicante
www.natouralds.com

Baum
Marta Barrera Altemir
Born in Sevilla , Spain, in 1979
She lives and works in Sevilla
Javier Caro Domínguez
Born in Sevilla , Spain, in 1979
He lives and works in Sevilla
Miguel Gentil Fernández
Born in Sevilla, Spain, in 1979
He lives and works in Sevilla
www.baumarquitectura.com

IAAC
Areti Markopoulou
Born in Thessaloniki, Greece, in
1980
She lives and works in Barcelona,
Spain
Marco Ingrassia
Born in Palermo, Italy, in 1988
He lves and works in Barcelona,
Spain
Diego Pajarito
Born in Bogotá, Colombia, in 1982
He lives and works in Barcelona,
Spain
Aurel Richard
Born in Paris, France, in 1991
He lives and works in Barcelona,
Spain
Raquel Villodrés
Born in Barcelona, Spain, in 1983
She lives and works in Barcelona
Starsk Lara
Born in Maracay, Venezuela, in 1981
She lives and works in Barcelona,
Spain
Angelos Chronis
Born in Kalamata, Greece, in 1980

He lives and works in Barcelona, Spain

Alejandro Cantera López
Born in Madrid, Spain, in 1990
He lives and works in Madrid, Spain

Nomad Garden
Sergio Rodríguez Estévez
Born in Huelva, Spain, in 1978
He lives and works in Sevilla, Spain
María Salas Mendoza Muro
Born in Huesca, Spain, in 1978
She lives and works in Sevilla, Spain
Francisco José Pazos García
Born in Santiago de Compostela, Spain, in 1980
He lives and works in Sevilla, Spain
Rubén Alonso Mallén
Born in Barcelona, Spain, in 1973
He lives and works in Sevilla, Spain
Esperanza Moreno Cruz
Born in Sevilla, Spain, in 1976
She lives and works in Sevilla
www.antropoloops.com

GarciaGerman Arquitectos
Jacobo García-Germán Vázquez
Born in Madrid, Spain, in 1974
He lives and works in Madrid, Spain
Raquel Díaz de la Campa Arias
Born in Léon, Spain in 1989
She lives and works in Madrid, Spain
Liguel López Ruiz
Born in Madrid, Spain, in 1990
He lives and works in Madrid
Marta Roldán Zahonero
Born in Madrid, Spain, in 1995
She lives and works in Madrid
www.garciagerman.com

Carmen Moreno Álvarez
Born in Granada, Spain, in 1976
She lives and works in Granada

Pez Estudio
Maé Durant Vidal
Born in Lima, Perú, in 1981
She lives and works in Madrid, Spain
Elisa de los Reyes García López
Born in Cangas del Nárcea, Spain, in 1981
She lives and works in Bilbao, Spain
Javier Pérez Contonente

Born in Madrid, Spain, in 1977
He lives and works in Madrid
Xabier Polledo Arrizabalaga
Born in Lemoa, Spain, in 1990
He lives and works in Bilbao, Spain

Sebastián Arquitectos Slp
Sergio Sebastián Franco
Born in Calatayud, Spain, in 1976
He lives and works in Zaragoza, Spain
www.sebastianarquitectos.com

Cuac Arquitectura
Tomás García Píriz
Born in Granada, Spain, in 1978
He lives and works in Granada, Spain
Francisco Javier Castellano Pulido
Born in Granada, Spain, in 1975
He lives and works in Granada
www.cuacarquitectura.com

Julien Fajardo
Born in Avignon, France, in 1981
He lives and works in Paris, France

Christophe Beauvez
Born in Brussels, Belgium, in 1982
He lives and works in Brussels

Sara San Gregorio
Born in Madrid, Spain, in 1984
She lives and works in Madrid

Ana Mombiedro
Born in Toledo, Spain, in 1987
She lives and works in Palma, Spain

Alicia Gutiérrez Fernández
Born in Santander, Spain, in 1983
She lives and works in Santander

Alexandre Dubor
Born in Paris, France, in 1986
He lives and works in Barcelona, Spain

Edouard Cabay
Born in Brussels, Belgium, in 1979
He lives and works in Barcelona, Spain

Kunaljit Chadha
Born in Nasik, India, in 1992
Lives and works in Barcelona, Spain

Mathilde Marengo
Born in Wollongong, Australia, in 1984
She lives and works in Barcelona, Spain

Chenta Tsai Tseng
Born in Taipei, Taiwan, in 1991
He lives and works in Madrid, Spain

SWITZERLAND
p. 121

Fabrice Aragno
Born in Neuchâtel, Switzerland, in 1970.
He lives and works in Lausanne, Switzerland

Mounir Ayoub
Born in Tunis, Tunisia in 1980.
He lives and works in Geneva, Switzerland

Vanessa Lacaille
Born in Paris, France, in 1980.
She lives and works in Geneva, Switzerland

Pierre Szczepski
Born in Caen, France, in 1991.
He lives and works in Geneva, Switzerland

THAILAND
p. 123

Boonserm Premthada
Born in Bangkok, Thailand, in 1966.
He lives and works in Bangkok

THREE BRITISH MOSQUES
p. 141

Shahed Saleem
Born in London, UK in 1971.
He lives and works in London

AIR/ARIA/AIRE_CATALONIA IN VENICE
p. 147

300.000 Km/s
Founded in Barcelona in 2014
Mar Santamaria Varas
Pablo Martínez
300000kms.net

CHARLOTTE PERRIAND AND I'. CONVERGING DESIGNS BY FRANK GEHRY AND CHARLOTTE PERRIAND
p. 149

Frank Gehry
Born in Toronto, Canada, in 1929
He lives and works in Los Angeles, California, USA

Charlotte Perriand
Paris, France 1903 - Paris, France 1999

CONNECTIVITIES: LIVING BEYOND THE BOUNDARIES – MACAO AND THE GREATER BAY AREA
p. 151

Ka Tat Chan Born in Macao, People's Republic of China, in 1984
He lives and works in Macao

Chi Hong Che Born in Macao, People's Republic of China, in 1990
He lives and works in Macao

Ting Fong Ho Born in Macao, People's Republic of China, in 1990
He lives and works in Macao

Man Si Lao Born in Macao, People's Republic of China, in 1986 She lives and works in Macao

HAKKA EARTHEN HOUSES ON VARIATION-CO-OPERATIVE LIVING, ART AND MIGRATION ARCHITECTURE IN CHINA
p. 153

An Haifeng
Born in Xianyang, People's Republic of China, in 1980
He lives and works in Nanning,People's Republic of China

Fu Zhongwang
Born in Wuhan, People's Republic of China, in 1956
He lives and works in Wuhan

Gu Xiong
Born in Chongqing, People's Republic of China, in 1953
He lives and works in Vancouver, Canada

He Duoling
Born in Chengdu, People's Republic of China, in 1948
He lives and works in Chengdu

Jiao Xingtao
Born in Chengdu, People's Republic of China, in 1970
He lives and works in Chongqing, People's Republic of China

Li Chuan
Born in Chongqing, People's Republic of China, in 1971
He lives and works in Chongqing

Li Xiangming
Born in Handan, People's Republic of China, in 1952
He lives and works in Beijing and Guizhou, People's Republic of China

Shi Jindian
Born in Yunnan, People's Republic of China, in 1953
He lives and works in Chengdu, People's Republic of China

Ye Fang
Born in Suzhou, People's Republic of China, in 1962
He lives and works in Suzhou

Ying Tianqi
Born in Anhui, People's Republic of China, in 1949
He lives and works in Shenzhen, People's Republic of China

Zhu Cheng
Born in Chengdu, People's Republic of China, in 1946
He lives and works in Chengdu

LIANGHEKOU
p. 155

Aldo Aymonino
Born in Rome, Italy, in 1953
He lives and works in Rome and Venice, Italy

Giuseppe Caldarola
Born in Bari, Italy, in 1979
He lives and works in Bari and Venice, Italy

Dongzhu Chu
Born in Mianzhu, People's Republic of China, in 1975
He lives and works in Chongqing, People's Republic of China

Enrico Fontanari
Born in Padua, Italy, in 1952
He lives and works in Venice, Italy

Cong Gong
Born in Weifang, People's Republic of China, in 1989
He lives and works in Chongqing, People's Republic of China

Baofeng Li
Born in Jilin, People's Republic of China, in 1956
He lives and works in Wuhan, People's Republic of China

Lin Qin
Born in LueYang, People's Republic of China, in 1971
She lives and works in Chongqing, People's Republic of China

Aihua Shao
Born in Wufeng, People's Republic of China, in 1973
He lives and works in Xuan'en, People's Republic of China

Shikuang Tang
Born in Wuhan, People's Republic of China, in 1982
He lives and works in Wuhan

Yuanwen Yao
Born in Wufeng, People's Republic of China, in 1969
He lives and works in Xuan'en, People's Republic of China

Chuan Wang
Born in Shaoxing, People's Republic of China, in 1989
He lives and works in Nanjing, People's Republic of China

Tong Wang
Born in Shandong, People's Republic of China, in 1982
He lives and works in Wuhan, People's Republic of China

Tong Zhang
Born in Hangzhou, People's Republic of China, in 1969
He lives and works in Nanjing, People's Republic of China

MUTUALITIES
p. 157

LAAS – Life as a Service
Founded in Singapore, in 2019
www.lifeasaservice.org

NOT VITAL. SCARCH
p. 159

Not Vital
Born in Sent, Switzerland in 1948
He Lives and works in Sent, Switzerland, Rio de Janeiro, Brazil, and Beijing, China.
notvital.com

PRIMITIVE MIGRATION FROM/TO TAIWAN
p. 161

Divooe Zein Architects
Established in Taipei, Taiwan in 2003

siu siu – Lab of Primitive Senses
Established in Taipei, Taiwan in 2014

TROPICALIA.
ARCHITECTURE, MATERIALS, INNOVATIVE SYSTEMS
p. 173

Coldefy
Founded in Lille, France, in 2006
Established in Lille and Paris, France, Shanghai and Hong Kong, People's Republic of China
www.caau.fr

17. Mostra Internazionale di Architettura
How will we live together?

La Biennale di Venezia
Editorial Activities and Web

Head
Flavia Fossa Margutti

Editorial Coordination
Maddalena Pietragnoli

Editorial Team
Francesca Dolzani
Giulia Gasparato
Elisa Testori

Graphic Design
Omnivore, Inc.

Editorial Realisation
Liberink srls, Padova
Coordination
Stefano Turon
Layout
Livio Cassese
Copy editing
Rosanna Alberti
Caterina Vettore

*Translations
and English language copy editing*
alphaville
traduzioni e servizi editoriali

Photolithography and Print
Graficart, Resana (TV)

Printed on

Paper made from cellulose from environmentally respectful, socially useful, and economically sustainable forests, production and supply chains, and other controlled sources

*9788836648597
DISTRIBUTED BY SILVANA EDITORIALE*

La Biennale di Venezia
First Edition May 2021